Linking Wilderness Research and Management

Volume 4 — Understanding and Managing Invasive Plants in Wilderness and Other Natural Areas:

An Annotated Reading List

I0447017

Series Editor:
Vita Wright, Research Application Program Director,
Aldo Leopold Wilderness Research Institute, Missoula, MT 59807
Rocky Mountain Research Station
U.S. Department of Agriculture, Forest Service

Authors:
Sophie Osborn, Ecology Specialist[a]
Vita Wright, Program Director
Brett Walker, Ecology Specialist[b]
Amy Cilimburg, Ecology Specialist[c]
Alison Perkins, Research Assistant

Research Application Program
Aldo Leopold Wilderness Research Institute, Missoula, MT 59807
Rocky Mountain Research Station
U.S. Department of Agriculture, Forest Service

[a] Currently, Field Manager, California Condor Restoration
Project, The Peregrine Fund, P.O. Box 6115, Marble
Canyon, AZ 86036.

[b] Currently, Ph.D. Degree Candidate, University of
Montana, Missoula, MT 59812.

[c] Currently, Researcher, Landbird Monitoring Project,
University of Montana, Missoula, MT 59812.

USDA Forest Service
General Technical Report RMRS-GTR-79-vol. 4.

September 2002

Preface

Federal land management agencies have recognized the importance of incorporating the best available scientific knowledge into management decisions. However, both managers and researchers have struggled to identify effective processes for accomplishing this objective. The Aldo Leopold Wilderness Research Institute's Research Application Program works toward understanding barriers to the use of science in management and develops ways to make relevant scientific information more accessible. Managers can base their decisions on the best available scientific knowledge only if they are aware of current and relevant science and how it fits into their management goals.

The Linking Wilderness Research and Management series of annotated reading lists was developed to help land managers and others access scientific information relevant to protecting and restoring wilderness and similarly managed lands, as well as protecting the myriad values associated with such lands. References in these reading lists have been categorized to draw attention to the relevance of each publication, and then organized to provide a logical framework for addressing the issue. Each volume begins with references necessary to understand the overall issue, and then provides references useful for identifying management goals, understanding influences on those goals, and finally, for selecting and implementing management approaches. For example, this Invasive Plant volume begins with sections on the problem of invasive plants in wilderness and other natural areas, invasive plant ecology overviews, and the factors that contribute to plant invasions. It then covers the effects of invasive plants on ecosystem processes, plant communities, and wildlife, and finishes with sections that include management considerations for preventing invasions, predicting potential spread, finding, mapping, and monitoring invasions, controlling invasive plants, and restoration. Within each section, articles have been annotated to clarify their relevance to that section and to highlight their relevance to wilderness management.

These reading lists were designed to serve a wide audience. First, each list introduces generalists to the breadth of factors that should be considered when addressing a management issue. These volumes also enable specialists to maintain familiarity with research relevant to their discipline but outside their area of expertise. For instance, this Invasive Plants volume may be useful to a botanist who specializes in protecting rare species but is not familiar with the invasive plant literature. For those generally familiar with the concepts, this series facilitates access to literature that can add depth to their conceptual knowledge. Rather than produce comprehensive bibliographies, which may be unwieldy for those with limited time, the authors included overviews, the most current examples of literature addressing pertinent concepts, and frequently cited classic publications. These lists can provide a starting point for readers interested in more detail on specific subjects to conduct their own literature reviews.

To facilitate access to these lists and enable us to update them, the lists are also available through the Aldo Leopold Wilderness Research Institute's Web site (http://leopold.wilderness.net/resapp.htm). The Leopold Institute is a Federal interagency research institute that focuses on ecological and social science research needed to sustain wilderness ecosystems and wilderness values. I hope this series will help sustain wilderness, similarly managed lands, and associated values by enabling managers, policymakers, educators, user groups, and others to access the best available science on the topics covered.

—Vita Wright, Series Editor

Acknowledgments

We sincerely appreciate the time Jerry Asher, Angie Evenden, Jon Keeley, Peter Landres, Eric Lane, Lloyd Loope, David Parsons, Noel Pavlovic, and John Randall took from their busy schedules to review various earlier versions of this publication. Each of these individuals provided helpful comments that improved the overall quality of the document. Thanks also to Suzanne Lingle and Dave Ausband for their assistance in writing several of the final annotations. Additional funding was received from the U.S. Fish and Wildlife Service, the Bureau of Land Management, and the interagency Arthur Carhart National Wilderness Training Center.

Contents

INTRODUCTION 1

   TERMINOLOGY 1

   SCOPE 1

   ORGANIZATION 2

ANNOTATED READING LIST 3

I. INVASIVE PLANTS IN WILDERNESS AND OTHER NATURAL AREAS 5

II. INVASIVE PLANT ECOLOGY 9

   A. Overviews 9

   B. Understanding Plant Invasions 13
      1. Biological Characteristics of Invading Species 13
      2. Site Characteristics and Disturbance History 14
      3. Mediated Dispersal 22

   C. Effects of Invasive Plants 24
      1. Effects on Plant Communities and Ecosystem Processes 24
      2. Effects on Wildlife 29

III. INVASIVE PLANT MANAGEMENT 33

   A. Management Planning 33

   B. Preventing Invasions 35

   C. Predicting Invasive Potential, Spread, and Distribution 36

   D. Finding, Mapping, and Monitoring Invasive Plants 39

   E. Control and Eradication 41
      1. Developing and Prioritizing Control Strategies 41
      2. Biological Control 45
      3. Chemical Control 48
      4. Mechanical and Manual Control 50
      5. Other Control Methods: Fire and Grazing 51

   F. Restoration 52

IV. ADDITIONAL RESOURCES 55

   A. Sample Environmental Impact Statements (EIS) 55

   B. Online Resources 56
      1. Databases 56
      2. Other Online Resources 57

   C. Cooperative Weed Management Areas 59

AUTHOR INDEX 60

INDEX OF PLANTS AND SELECTED VEGETATION TYPES 63

INTRODUCTION

Invasive, nonnative plants are recognized as a significant and growing threat to natural ecosystems worldwide. Invasive plants disrupt natural conditions by changing the physical, chemical, and biological attributes of the areas they invade. This often leads to changes in communities of native species, shifts in ecological interactions, alteration of large scale ecosystem processes, and ultimately, a reduction in native biodiversity.

Although wilderness areas are widely valued for their native flora and fauna and intact natural processes, these core aspects of wilderness are susceptible to, and increasingly threatened by, nonnative plant invasions. Most wilderness areas contain at least some invasive plants. In many wildernesses, invasive plants are already altering natural conditions. In addition to preventing new invasions and mapping and monitoring existing invasions, wilderness and other natural area managers are now faced with the complex problem of deciding how, when, and where to control such invasions.

Controlling invasions in wilderness settings can be controversial, especially in Congressionally designated wilderness. The Wilderness Act of 1964 [Public Law 88 577] states that wilderness should be "protected and managed so as to preserve its natural conditions." However, the Act also mandates that wilderness be "untrammeled," or unmanipulated. Based on this language, wilderness areas historically have been managed in ways that minimize intentional human intervention. The increasing spread and impacts of invasive, nonnative plants, along with the fact that most known control efforts are intentionally manipulative, and that invasions in the absence of control will continue to decrease the naturalness of wilderness ecosystems, are leading to new challenges and conflicts in how to manage for and preserve natural conditions.

Federal policy mandates that agency management decisions consider the best available science. This requires managers to be aware of current research regarding the ecology of invasive plants as well as available management options. Gathering the background information needed to properly manage invasive plants can be a formidable task. This is a large and rapidly expanding field, and the sheer volume of research and the number of disparate literature sources in which it is published can be overwhelming.

To facilitate an understanding of this topic, and ultimately the ability to make informed management decisions, we have compiled an annotated reading list that covers those aspects of invasive plant ecology and management most relevant to wilderness and other areas managed for their ecological values. Our intent is to (1) promote an improved understanding of the ecology and impacts of invasive plants, (2) to familiarize managers with current literature on various management approaches, and (3) to facilitate access to relevant references.

TERMINOLOGY

Various terms and definitions for nonnative, invasive species can be found in the literature. According to Reichard and White (2001) an invasive plant is "…one that has or is likely to spread into native flora and managed plant systems, develop self sustaining populations, and become dominant or disruptive (or both) to those systems." Executive Order 13112 generally concurs by defining an "invasive species" as a species that is (1) nonnative (or alien) to the ecosystem under consideration and (2) whose introduction causes or is likely to cause economic or environmental harm or harm to human health. Within this document we have used these definitions and concentrated on literature about nonnative invasive plants. Nonetheless, within each annotation, we have generally repeated the terminology used by the author(s) (for example, exotic, nonindigenous, nonnative, invasive, weed). We have also retained the common and scientific names as the authors presented them, in an attempt to avoid confusion over regional differences in the use of species names.

SCOPE

There is a plethora of published information about invasive plants. Rather than focus on the body of literature that is aimed at understanding and managing *individual* species, much of which is already accessible through a variety of sources, we have chosen to develop a list of references that addresses concepts that must be considered when managing invasive plants in wilderness and other natural areas. For instance, rather than include references about control techniques targeted at each species, we have included papers that we hope will help managers make decisions about when and where to consider using manipulative control strategies, and to help weigh the potential unintended consequences of these manipulations against the potential costs of allowing invasions to continue to exist and spread. While the reading list does not address individual species comprehensively, we include publications that are focused on individual species as illustrations of pertinent concepts that may be applicable to other species or other ecosystems.

We have included overviews of the topics included in this list; many of these emphasize the same messages. We have used the most recent literature we could find to illustrate pertinent concepts, with the idea that recent publications and overviews would cite older papers and enable readers interested in more depth to conduct their own literature reviews. Our goal was to review literature covering a wide range of issues that are important for understanding and managing invasive plants and for which publications exist. We did this rather than going into depth on any particular issue. Had we added depth, we would have defeated our purpose of providing readers with a manageable list of references. While the list will become outdated, we hope the synthesis of concepts will be useful for a long time.

The sources cited here represent a significant portion of the recent invasive plant literature. The references listed in sections on topics for which little research has been published (for example, effects on wildlife) are more comprehensive than references in sections for which publications are abundant (for example, understanding plant invasions, or biological and chemical control). Additionally, for sections that have an abundance of literature, we have only included references that provide recent overviews or present information intended to help managers decide when and where to apply management approaches in wilderness.

In addition to providing insight into general invasive species ecology, this list provides information about unique issues related to understanding and managing invasive plants in wilderness settings. These include factors that contribute to plant invasions in wilderness, the current status of plant invasions in wilderness, and management considerations specific to wilderness and other natural areas.

Overall, this reading list provides an introduction to the literature on the ecology and management of invasive, nonnative plants. We attempted to compile and organize references in a way that will be useful to those interested in wilderness management and research. Although this list focuses primarily on the North American literature, readers should be aware that a great deal of research on invasive plants has also been conducted elsewhere, particularly in Australia and South Africa.

ORGANIZATION

This reading list is organized as a framework for addressing invasive plant issues in wilderness and other natural areas. The reading list begins with an overview of unique concerns related to understanding and managing invasive plants in wilderness settings. The papers in this section describe the threats that plant invasions currently pose to wilderness and other reserves worldwide that are managed for their natural values. These papers also detail the urgency of addressing wilderness invasions. The next section, part II, provides references that explain the factors that contribute to plant invasions, as well as their effects on native species, communities, and ecosystems. This section includes topics that provide the foundation of understanding upon which management decisions can be made. References in part III explore options for managing invasive plants, ranging from preventing, predicting, and mapping to controlling invasions and restoring affected areas. Finally, in part IV, we list additional resources, including examples of Federal Environmental Impact Statements that address invasive plants in designated U.S. wilderness areas, a list of online databases and other relevant Web sites, and information about Cooperative Weed Management Areas.

For each of the major sections within parts I through IV, we provide a short summary of the information contained in that section along with an annotated list of key references. Within each section, publications are alphabetized by author. Some references are relevant to multiple topics and so are listed in multiple places. While this may seem redundant to readers of the entire document, it is meant to assist readers who go directly to certain sections. The full annotation is given only once under the section we deem to be most pertinent. In other relevant sections, we list the citation and cross reference to the section in which the full annotation can be found.

Citations are formatted in accordance with the original works. As a result, author names do not necessarily appear in the same format throughout the reading list. Because plant common names are not always exclusive and may refer to different species in different regions, we only include scientific names when they appear in the original reference. In addition, we used the scientific and common names as they were used in the original article; we did not change species names to reflect current classification schemes. Readers can refer to the U.S. Department of Agriculture's Web site PLANTS (http://plants.usda.gov/cgi bin/) for an up to date and standardized list of common and scientific plant names.

ANNOTATED READING LIST

I. Invasive Plants in Wilderness and Other Natural Areas

This section includes papers that articulate problems di rectly associated with invasive plants and Federally designated wilderness areas, National Parks, Nature Conservancy pre serves, and other natural areas. Many of the papers published convey the same messages: in spite of goals to maintain natu ral conditions, invasive plants are threatening wilderness eco systems, and further degradation will only be avoided by acting soon. Some authors draw attention to the urgency of this issue (Hester 1991, Kummerow 1992, Lesica and others 1993, Asher and Harmon 1995, Randall 1996) and review the general prob lem (Marion and others 1986, Loope and others 1988, Macdonald and Frame 1988, Macdonald and others 1988, Usher 1988, Loope 1992, Cole and Landres 1996). Others address specific issues related to managing invasive plants in natural areas, including the ecological impacts of invasive plants (Bratton 1982, Asher and Harmon 1995, Dudley and Collins 1995), management concerns (Dudley and Embury 1995, Randall 1995, 1996), and research needs (Cole and Landres 1996, Marler 2000, Randall 2000) specific to wilder ness. In addition, Marler (2000) reviews the status of invasive plants in Federally designated wilderness areas, and Randall (1995) reviews the status in Nature Conservancy preserves.

Asher, Jerry A.; Harmon, David W. 1995. Invasive exotic plants are destroying the naturalness of U.S. wilderness areas. International Journal of Wilderness. 1(2): 35 37.

Annotation: The rapid spread of invasive nonnative plants into wilderness ecosystems necessitates management respond quickly to prevent the degradation of these areas. After briefly addressing the ability of exotic plants to invade undisturbed areas and the mechanisms by which these weeds spread into wilderness, the authors discuss and give examples of the ex ponential increase of these plants on public lands. Because such invasions violate the mandates, policies, and goals of wilderness management, the authors exhort managers to re spond quickly to this threat, including using herbicides when they are the only effective means of control. Finally, the au thors outline several potential strategies for protecting the natu ralness of wilderness. They suggest that information about the threat of exotic plant invasions should also be incorporated into the national Leave No Trace Program.

Bratton, Susan P. 1982. The effects of exotic plant and ani mal species on nature preserves. Natural Areas Journal. 2(3): 3 13.

Annotation: Exotic species may have irreversible impacts on nature preserves. The author first outlines reasons why pre serves are vulnerable to introduced species and discusses the difficulties managers may face when trying to define exotic species. She then reviews and provides examples of ecosys tem level effects of nonnative species invasions in preserves.

Cheater, Mark. 1992. Alien invasion. Nature Conservancy. 42(5): 24 29.

Annotation: This paper presents a brief introduction to the invasive nonnative plant problem, with an emphasis on Na ture Conservancy preserves. In particular, it focuses on three invasive aliens that are displacing native plants: tall fescue (*Festuca arundinacea*), water hyacinth (*Eichhornia* spp.), and Canada thistle (*Cirsium arvense*). The issue of chemical and bio logical control of these and other species is briefly discussed.

Cole, David N.; Landres, Peter B. 1996. Threats to wilder ness ecosystems: impacts and research needs. Ecological Applications. 6(1): 168 184.

Annotation: The introduction and invasion of alien species is identified as one of seven of the most significant threats to wilderness ecosystems. The authors discuss ways in which exotic species can affect both ecosystem level processes and the distribution and abundance of native species. In addition, they identify general invasion patterns based on reviews of the effects of nonnative species on nature reserves. After men tioning a variety of activities both within and outside of wil derness areas that facilitate the spread of invasive exotics into wilderness, the authors raise questions in the hopes of stimu lating further research on this topic.

Dudley, T.; Collins, B. 1995. Biological invasions in Cali fornia wetlands—the impacts and control of nonindigenous species in natural areas. Oakland, CA: Pacific Institute for Studies in Development, Environment, and Security. 57 p. *(Note: This document can be obtained by ordering it from http:/ /www.pacinst.org/PubsOrderForm.html or by calling 510 251 1600.)*

Annotation: The authors surveyed 52 natural area managers in California to assess the current status, impacts, and management of invasive species on aquatic, wetland, and riparian habitats. All managers had problems with invasive plants, and most reported that a lack of funding prevented them from adequately monitoring and controlling known populations of invasive species. Low elevation and coastal areas were most heavily impacted. Plants with widely dispersed propagules and broad ecological tolerances were the largest threats. Rapid eradication of known invasive species was extremely effective at preventing their establishment. The authors conclude that managers and scientists need to collaborate on studies of invasive species ecology in order to institute effective monitoring and control programs. They also suggest that new legislation is needed to improve the regulation and importation of invasive species that threaten natural areas, rather than focusing only on those that threaten agriculture. Educating the public about the threat of invasive species is also a critical part of successfully implementing a control program and enforcing laws geared toward preventing the spread of invasive species. In an appendix, the authors present a model law to act as the basis for future legislation and a little known Federal executive order mandating that Federal, state, and local government agencies restrict the introduction of nonnative species.

Dudley, T.; Embury, M. 1995. Nonindigenous species in wilderness areas: the status and impacts of livestock and game species in designated wilderness in California. Oakland, CA: Pacific Institute for Studies in Development, Environment, and Security. 38 p. *(Note: This document can be obtained by ordering it from http://www.pacinst.org/ PubsOrderForm.html or by calling 510 251 1600.)*

Annotation: Although this study focuses primarily on the status and impacts of introduced animals (livestock and game species), rather than plants, it highlights several controversies surrounding wilderness management that relate directly to problems with invasive exotic plants. First, livestock grazing may facilitate exotic plant invasions by disturbing and eroding soils, particularly in invasion prone streamside areas. Second, few wilderness areas have systematic ecological monitoring programs, so the actual distribution, abundance, and impacts of introduced plants in most California wilderness areas remains unknown. Third, many wilderness managers express concerns over the impacts of recreational pack stock because of their potential to disturb soil and transport invasive plant seeds.

Hester, F. Eugene. 1991. The U.S. National Park Service experience with exotic species. Natural Areas Journal. 11: 127 128.

Annotation: A survey conducted by the National Park Service (NPS) in 1986 and 1987 found that exotic plants were the most commonly reported threat to park resources. Eighty eight parks reported having problems with nonnative plants. Therefore, this paper outlines the NPS's policy with regards to nonnative species in U.S. parks. Examples are provided of the monetary costs of managing exotics and factors are identified that will be essential to the future successful management of nonnative species, including funding, agency cooperation, research, monitoring, and education.

Kummerow, Max. 1992. Weeds in wilderness: a threat to biodiversity. Western Wildlands. 18: 12 17; Summer.

Annotation: The author first describes the increasing presence of weeds in Montana's wilderness areas and the tendency of these plants to spread at exponential rates, and then uses examples from around the world to depict possible long term outcomes of the introduction of nonnative species into new areas. Kummerow next lists a number of preventative measures, including steps to reduce the transport of seeds into wilderness and to mitigate disturbances that promote the spread of weeds. In addition, he compares various control measures and concludes that herbicide spraying is probably the only practical means of weed control in wilderness. Finally, Kummerow emphasizes the importance of early action and illustrates the danger of delaying efforts.

Lesica, Peter; Ahlenslager, Kathleen; Desanto, Jerry. 1993. New vascular plant records and the increase of exotic plants in Glacier National Park, Montana. Madroño. 40(2): 126 131.

Annotation: At least 57 species of exotic plants were present in Glacier National Park in 1920, and since then, the number has grown at an accelerating rate. The authors report 14 new additions to the nonnative flora and show a correlation between the proliferation of weeds and the increased visitation to the park. Their findings suggest that monitoring the success of new invaders is an increasingly important task for preserve managers. The control of these exotics will be an ever growing challenge, particularly in those areas that have high visitation.

Loope, Lloyd L. 1992. An overview of problems with introduced plant species in National Parks and biosphere reserves in the United States. In: Stone, Charles P.; Smith, Clifford W.; Tunison, J. Timothy, eds. Alien plant invasions in native ecosystems of Hawai'i: management and research. Honolulu, HA: Cooperative National Park Resources Studies Unit. University of Hawaii Press: 3 28. *(Note: This book can be obtained by calling 808 956 8255.)*

Annotation: After outlining some of the potential threats that exotic plants pose to nature reserves, Loope presents an overview of the nature and the severity of the effects of exotic plants in different biogeographic regions. The author also discusses possible reasons why islands (and particularly those in the state of Hawai'i) are especially susceptible to invasions. In an appendix, the author summarizes the status of exotics in individual U.S. Biosphere Reserves based on a survey of managers.

Loope, Lloyd L.; Sanchez, Peter G.; Tarr, Peter W.; Loope, Walter L.; Anderson, Richard L. 1988. Biological invasions of arid land nature reserves. Biological Conservation. 44: 95 118.

Annotation: This paper uses five case studies to examine the effects of exotics on nature reserves in arid environments. In general, arid reserves do not seem as susceptible to invasion as other types of biomes, except along their watercourses. However, an arid island reserve experienced more extensive invasions than did the continental reserves. Invasive plants (for example, *Tamarix*) along perennial or intermittent water courses in arid reserves displace the native vegetation and often lower water tables, thereby reducing habitat for aquatic life and water sources for wildlife.

Macdonald, I. A. W.; Frame, G. W. 1988. The invasion of introduced species into nature reserves in tropical savannas and dry woodlands. Biological Conservation. 44: 67 93.

Annotation: Five case studies illustrate the effects invasive nonnative species can have on nature reserves in tropical sa vannas and dry woodlands. Possible threats from invasive plants include changes in fire regimes and in relationships be tween native fruit trees and frugivores. Plant invasions appear to be less widespread in the drier portions of these biomes than in moister regions, perhaps because fire and herbivory by large animals limit the successful spread of these invaders in drier habitats. In moist portions of the reserves, invasive, scrambling shrubs are a serious problem. Initiating control measures early in the invasion process is critical for preserv ing such habitats. Of all the habitat types found in these re serves, aquatic habitats were the most threatened by invasions of trees, shrubs, herbs, and aquatic macrophytes. The control of exotics that disperse into nature reserves by floating down rivers remains a critical issue.

Macdonald, I. A. W.; Graber, D. M.; DeBenedetti, S.; Groves, R. H.; Fuentes, E. R. 1988. Introduced species in nature reserves in Mediterranean-type climate regions of the world. Biological Conservation. 44: 37 66.

Annotation: Nature reserves in the Mediterranean type cli matic regions of the world are experiencing invasion by non native species. Overall, invasibility is greater in small reserves than large ones. Small reserves in urban areas are especially at risk of invasion by nonnative plants. The major invasions into Mediterranean type reserves have been primarily by an nual grasses from Europe and the Mediterranean basin. How ever, these reserves also appear to be especially susceptible to invasions by nonnative species from elsewhere on their own continents. Invasions in Mediterranean type reserves altered fire regimes and reduced densities of the native biota. Because these types of reserves appear to be highly susceptible to in vasions, the authors recommend that managers minimize the number of accidental introductions, avoid practices that alter fire regimes and herbivory under which the native biota have evolved, and prevent intentional introductions, even from ar eas on the same continent.

Macdonald, Ian A. W.; Loope, Lloyd L.; Usher, Michael B.; Hamann, O. 1989. Wildlife conservation and the inva sion of nature reserves by introduced species: a global per spective. In: Drake, J. A.; Mooney, H. A.; di Castri, F.; Groves, R. H.; Kruger, F. J.; Rejmánek, M.; Williamson, M., eds. Bio logical invasions: a global perspective. Chichester, England: John Wiley and Sons: 215 255.

Annotation: See section II.C.1. Page 26.

Marion, Jeffrey L.; Cole, David N.; Bratton, Susan P. 1986. Exotic vegetation in wilderness areas. In: Lucas, R. C., ed. Proceedings: national wilderness research conference: current research; 1985 July 23 26; Fort Collins, CO. Gen. Tech. Rep. INT 212. Ogden, UT: U.S. Department of Agriculture, Forest Service, Intermountain Research Station: 114 120.

Annotation: This paper outlines reasons that wilderness man agers should be concerned about nonnative plant invasions. Non native plants represent deviations from natural conditions, provide visitors with a false image of an area's natural vegetation,

displace native species, and greatly alter ecosystem processes. They discuss how exotic plants are introduced to and disperse within wilderness areas and outline steps managers can take to minimize and control the spread of exotics.

Marler, Marilyn. 2000. A survey of exotic plants in Fed eral wilderness areas. In: Cole, David N.; McCool, Stephen F.; Borrie, William T.; O'Loughlin, Jennifer, comps. Wilder ness science in a time of change conference Volume 5: Wil derness ecosystems, threats, and management; 1999 May 23 27; Missoula, MT. Proc. RMRS P 15 VOL 5. Ogden, UT: U.S. Department of Agriculture, Forest Service, Rocky Moun tain Research Station: 318 327.

Annotation: To determine the current status of invasive plants and their management in Federally designated wilderness, Marler conducted a survey of all designated U.S. wilderness area managers. Approximately 50 percent of managers re sponded to the survey. Among respondents, 15 percent con sidered invasive weeds a top management priority for their area. However, only one third of the locations had monitoring programs in place to determine the extent of the invasion prob lem, and approximately 40 percent did not monitor for inva sive plants, often due to difficult access (especially in Alaska) and a lack of sufficient funding. Responses are summarized by region/biome. The author discusses mechanisms of spread into wilderness areas reported by managers, appropriate man agement responses when exotics are found, and continuing threats to wilderness from invasive plants. Current research needs include discovering how invasive plants respond to natu ral disturbances in wilderness and the ecological impacts of naturalized invasives. Due to the low response rate and the lack of widespread monitoring programs, the true status of invasive weeds in designated wilderness remains unknown. Although traditionally underfunded by government agencies, inventory and monitoring programs are most needed.

Randall, John M. 1995. Weeds and natural areas manage ment. In: Proceedings: sixteenth annual forest vegetation management conference; 1995 January 10 12; Sacramento, CA. Redding, CA: Shasta County Opportunity Center: 23 28.

Annotation: The author first presents a brief overview of how invasive nonnative plants threaten natural areas and biodiversity. He then discusses the results of a survey of Na ture Conservancy land managers assessing the current status and threat level of exotic weeds on Nature Conservancy pre serves. After citing specific examples of weed problems on these preserves and ways in which they are being addressed, Randall poses several questions that highlight some of the un knowns in weed management. Finally, he discusses ways of slowing the establishment of new weeds, describes the mis sion and accomplishments of the California Exotic Pest Plant Council, and outlines a five point plan for weed control in natural areas.

Randall, John M. 1996. Weed control for the preservation of biological diversity. Weed Technology. 10(2): 370 383.

Annotation: Invasive nonnative species pose a magnanimous threat to the world's ecosystems and communities, but terms as sociated with this phenomenon are often confusing. Randall de fines these terms, describes the ways in which exotic plants can displace native species and degrade biological communities (ecosystem effects, habitat dominance, hybridization with native species, promotion of nonnative animals), and discusses the extent of wildland weed problems in the United States. He also outlines a strategy that wildland managers can use to approach the control of exotic plants. In the end, Randall discusses a few of the unique problems associated with wildland weed control and poses a variety of related questions in the hopes of stimulating further research into wildland weeds.

Randall, John M. 2000. Improving management of nonnative invasive plants in wilderness and other natural areas. In: Cole, David N.; McCool, Stephen F.; Borrie, William T.; O'Loughlin, Jennifer, comps. Wilderness science in a time of change conference Volume 5: Wilderness ecosystems, threats, and management; 1999 May 23 27; Missoula, MT. Proc. RMRS P 15 VOL 5. Ogden, UT: U.S. Department of Agriculture, Forest Service, Rocky Mountain Research Station: 64 73.

Annotation: This article provides an excellent overview of recent research findings and future research directions in invasive plant ecology. The author first emphasizes that invasive weeds are the second most important threat to biological diversity in the world. He then reviews the causes, consequences, mechanisms, and ecological impacts of such invasions and examines the status of control and restoration efforts. Studies that quantify the positive and negative ecological impacts of control efforts are needed. In addition, managers need to make informed decisions about which invasives to prioritize for control and to use adaptive management strategies. Randall emphasizes the need for improved methods for preventing invasions, mapping, monitoring, and controlling invasive plants, and additional research on the ecological role of introduced plants in native ecosystems.

Usher, Michael B. 1988. Biological invasions of nature reserves: a search for generalisations. Biological Conservation. 44: 119 135.

Annotation: This is the final paper in the series edited by E. Duffey and M. B. Usher, and it focuses on biological invasions of nature reserves in different types of biomes. As such, it draws generalizations from the case studies presented in other papers. All reserves studied experienced invasions by nonnative species. Island reserves experienced the highest level of invasive exotic species (30 percent of the flora consists of nonnative invasive species), while savannas and dry woodlands had the lowest level of exotics (9 percent of the flora is composed of invasive nonnatives). The other biomes (Mediterranean and arid land) are intermediate. In these latter two biomes, smaller reserves have a greater level of exotics than do larger reserves. Management priorities in reserves have been given to invasives that threaten endemic species with extinction and to invasive species that have a strong landscape effect. Because increased visitation is correlated with an increased number of introduced species, expanding and unregulated tourism may be a threat to nature reserves. The author recommends that conservation managers monitor new invasions, initiate control operations early, reduce ecosystemwide disturbances that favor invasions, and follow a clearly defined long term management plan.

II. Invasive Plant Ecology

A. Overviews

The following publications offer broad overviews that in troduce readers to important concepts, patterns, and trends in the field of invasive plant ecology and management. Nontech nical overviews are provided by Cronk and Fuller (1995), the Office of Technology Assessment (1993), Randall (1997), and Westbrooks (1998). The remaining citations refer to overview articles, compilations of papers on invasive plant research, or conference proceedings that are valuable general references.

Baker, H. G. 1986. Patterns of plant invasion in North America. In: Mooney, Harold A.; Drake, James A., eds. Ecol ogy of biological invasions of North America and Hawaii. New York, NY: Springer Verlag: 44 57.

Annotation: This paper introduces the reader to nonnative plant invasions in North America. The author discusses the origins and modes of spreading weeds and describes different types of invading plants, providing numerous examples of both successful and unsuccessful introductions. The vulnerability and resistance of different types of ecosystems to invasion are also addressed. Two primary patterns of spread usually char acterize invasions: (1) the steady advance of a population, and (2) the scattering of "satellite" populations from an original introduction, followed by a filling in of the space between these populations. "Minor" (those with limited invasive po tential) and "major" weeds (those with high invasive poten tial) are contrasted and patterns of exotic plant invasions in relation to their native distribution and examples of sequen tial invasions (the displacement of one exotic species by an other) are discussed. Baker concludes with generalizations regarding invaders and the environments they colonize.

Baskin, Yvonne. 2002. A plague of rats and rubbervines. Washington, DC: Island Press. 377 p.

Annotation: Sponsored by the nongovernmental organization SCOPE (Scientific Committee on Problems of the Environ ment), this book was written to share the findings of SCOPE's Global Invasive Species Programme with the public. The Programme consists of a team of biologists, natural resource managers, economists, lawyers, and policymakers gathered to draw international attention to biological invasions and to help prevent, control or eradicate the introduction of invasive alien species. This easy read uses examples from around the world to put the invasion issue into a global context. After drawing the reader to an awareness of the problem, the author explores the extent and consequences of biological invasions and the human forces that continue to move species, deliber ately and accidentally, around the world. Most of the book chronicles examples of efforts to stop invaders and to pre serve invaded lands. Such efforts include attempts to predict which species will become successful invaders, early detec tion, and ecosystem restoration. The following themes are high lighted: biological invasions affect all social and economic sectors of all countries, and the "problem" is limited to the subset of imported species that "escape control and cause eco logical or economic harm."

Binggeli, Pierre. 1996. A taxonomic, biogeographical and ecological overview of invasive woody plants. Journal of Vegetation Science. 7: 121 124.

Annotation: This paper describes and summarizes the find ings of a database on invasive woody plant species. Based on 2045 biographical references, the database contains informa tion on 653 species from 110 families. Europe has the most recorded invasions by woody plants, followed by the Pacific islands, North America, New Zealand, and Australia. An equal number of invasive events have been reported from continents and oceanic islands. Among woody plants, the families Ro saceae (rose), Mimosaceae (mimosa), Papilionaceae (pea), and Pinaceae (pine) contain the largest number of invasive spe cies. While most invasions occur in highly disturbed habitats, natural communities are also susceptible. Forests are most vul nerable to invasions by woody plants. Invasive woody plants may be either insect pollinated or wind pollinated, and they typically have a wide range of fruit types, fruit and seed sizes, seeds per fruit, and dispersal agents.

Cox, George W. 1999. Alien species in North America and Hawaii: impacts on natural ecosystems. Washington, DC: Island Press. 387 p.

Annotation: Primarily focused on the Continental United States and Hawaii, this book includes chapters that describe the many plant, animal, and pathogen invasions and their impacts in the most seriously invaded regions of North America

(Eastern seaboard, West Coast bays and estuaries, Northern temperate lakes, Western rivers and streams, Eastern forests, Florida and Gulf lowlands, Plains and Intermontane grasslands, Western floodplains, Pacific States, and Hawaiian Islands). The author provides a thorough overview of the extensive impacts caused by invading species and reminds readers how exotic species are spread through human actions as well as the physical and biotic features of the continent's landscapes. In the latter part of the book, he reviews information about the factors that promote invasions and investigates potential long term ecological and evolutionary changes in invaded communities. He addresses economic impacts of exotics, evaluating efforts to control exotic species, discussing future options for integrated management, and examining public policy at a variety of levels. If a successful strategy for dealing with invaders is not devised, he warns that North America will "risk the extreme degradation of some of the world's most pristine natural ecosystems."

Cronk, Quentin C. B.; Fuller, Janice L. 1995. Plant invaders: the threat to natural ecosystems. New York, NY: Chapman and Hall. 256 p.

Annotation: Several international organizations joined effort to "draw attention to the growing threat of invasive plant species" in natural and seminatural ecosystems around the world. The book is one of the most up to date and readable reviews of invasive plant ecology for nonscientific audiences. In the first section, the authors discuss the geographic scope and threat of plant invasions, how they occur, global, taxonomic, and habitat specific patterns of invasion, and actions that can be taken to stop their spread. Several examples are used to illustrate each point. The second section of the book includes an in depth look at case studies of important invasive species in natural areas. This is followed by a representative (rather than comprehensive) list of invasive plant species from around the world. For each species, the authors provide a basic description of the plant, information about its native range, the regions it has invaded, and notes on its biology, ecology, and control.

Drake, J. A.; Mooney, H. A.; di Castri, F.; Groves, R. H.; Kruger, F. J.; Rejmánek, M.; Williamson, M. 1989. Biological invasions: a global perspective. Chichester, England: John Wiley and Sons. 525 p.

Annotation: This book, which evolved from the SCOPE (Scientific Committee on Problems of the Environment) program on the ecology of biological invasions, synthesizes much of the current knowledge on invasions worldwide. The 22 chapters (many of which are cited separately below) include a history of biological invasions (di Castri); patterns, extents, and modes of invasion by terrestrial (Heywood) and aquatic (Ashton and Mitchell) plants; and characteristics and consequences of invaded temperate grasslands (Mack), Mediterranean climate regions (Kruger and others), nature reserves (Macdonald and others), and islands (Loope and Mueller Dombois). Additional chapters relevant to plants include the effects of biological invasions on ecosystems (Ramakrishnan and Vitousek), attributes of invading terrestrial and vascular plants (Noble), mathematical models of invasion (Williamson), the invasibility of plant communities (Rejmánek), the role of disturbance (Hobbs), chance and timing in biological invasions (Crawley), and the control of invasive terrestrial plants (Groves). The last chapter provides an overview of the SCOPE program on biological invasions and some final generalizations about invasive species.

Elton, Charles S. 1958. The ecology of invasions by animals and plants. London, England: Methuen and Company. 181 p.

Annotation: Elton was the first to bring biological invasions to the forefront of ecology. Using a wide variety of examples, he illustrates how invasive nonnative species have disrupted global communities and ecosystems, and the ways in which humans have facilitated such changes. After presenting examples of continental, island, and ocean invasions, Elton addresses why certain species are successful invaders while others are not and why certain habitats are more vulnerable to invasion than others. This book does not focus specifically on plant invasions.

Heywood, Vernon H. 1989. Patterns, extents and modes of invasions by terrestrial plants. In: Drake, J. A.; Mooney, H. A.; di Castri, F.; Groves, R. H.; Kruger, F. J.; Rejmánek, M.; Williamson, M., eds. Biological invasions: a global perspective. Chichester, England: John Wiley and Sons: 31 60.

Annotation: This paper provides a summary of the world's most invasive plants, their biogeographical distributions, and the various factors that have facilitated such invasions. Most invasive families, genera, and species of plants worldwide are summarized and the extents of these invasions in each of the major biogeographic regions of the world are described. The ways in which humans have facilitated or promoted these invasions, and the historical phases during which most invasions have occurred, are described.

Lacey, John R.; Olson, Bret E. 1991. Environmental and economic impacts of noxious range weeds. In: James, Lynn F.; Evans, John O.; Ralphs, Michael H.; Child, R. Dennis, eds. Noxious range weeds. Boulder, CO: Westview Press: 5 16.

Annotation: In this paper, the authors examined the known impacts of Federally designated noxious weeds on rangelands. Noxious weeds reduce forage for valuable game species, such as elk and deer, and replace ecologically important native vegetation. In some areas, the impacts of noxious weeds can be severe and may even affect the economy of an entire region. Noxious weeds reduce the value of rangeland, negatively affect the health and market value of livestock, and increase operating and management costs for ranchers. The authors conclude that the most serious issue facing land managers, ranchers, and legislators is the lack of published information related to the impacts of noxious weeds.

Luken, James O.; Thieret, John W. 1997. Assessment and management of plant invasions. New York, NY: Springer Verlag. 456 p.

Annotation: This book focuses on evaluating the broad ecological impacts of nonnative plants and on managing such invasions in relation to conservation goals and ecosystem attributes. The book is divided into four sections: I. Human perceptions, II. Assessment of ecological interactions, III. Direct management, IV. Regulation and advocacy. The first section defines indigenous and nonindigenous species and assesses the potential ecological values of exotic plants. The next section focuses on factors promoting invasions, impacts of exotic plants on communities and ecosystems, and interactions between exotics and other agents of global change.

The management section includes ways to prioritize the management of invasive plants and various control methods for aquatic and terrestrial plants. The final section focuses on preventing plant introductions and on cooperative, interagency weed management efforts.

Monsen, Stephen B.; Kitchen, Stanley G., eds. 1994. Proceedings: ecology and management of annual rangelands; 1992 May 18–22; Boise, ID. Gen. Tech. Rep. INT GTR 313. Ogden, UT: U.S. Department of Agriculture, Forest Service, Intermountain Research Station. 416 p.

Annotation: These proceedings contain a variety of studies addressing the impacts and control of plant invasions on range lands, restoration of rangelands, and the biology of introduced annual grasses and native range plants. For example, Peters and Bunting (see annotation in II.C.1 Page 27) examine fire and annual grasses on the Snake River plain, and Monsen offers a list of plants useful in fire suppression on semiarid sites. Rosentreter discusses displacement of rare plants by invasive grasses. Novak addresses variation among cheatgrass populations, and with Pyke examines the role multiple introductions may have on invasion. Kennedy discusses the biological control of annual grasses.

Mooney, Harold A.; Drake, James A. 1986. Ecology of biological invasions of North America and Hawaii. New York, NY: Springer Verlag. 321 p.

Annotation: This book, which evolved from the SCOPE (Scientific Committee on Problems of the Environment) program investigating the ecology of biological invasions, focuses on biological invasions in North America and Hawaii. It is divided into six sections: I. Patterns of invasions: a systematic perspective, II. Attributes of invaders, III. Site characteristics promoting invasions and system impacts of invaders, IV. Modeling the invasion process, V. Biogeographic case histories, and VI. Control of invaders. The first section consists of four chapters summarizing patterns of invasions by different types of organisms (plant chapter is by Baker), while the next three chapters focus on characteristics of invaders (plant chapter by Bazzaz) and a discussion of genetically engineered organisms. The third section (three chapters, by Orian, Pimentel, and Vitousek) deals with mechanisms that facilitate invasions and their economic and ecological impacts. Section IV consists of one chapter on predicting invasions and rates of spread, while the four chapters in Section V describe case histories of invasions in the Intermountain West (Mack), South Florida (Ewel), Hawaii (Moulton and Pimm), and California (Mooney and others). The final chapter discusses the control of invaders.

Mooney, Harold A.; Hobbs, Richard J., eds. 2000. Invasive species in a changing world. Washington, DC: Island Press. 457 p.

Annotation: Invasive species are a global problem, a problem that will worsen with global change in climate, commerce, land use patterns, fire regimes, and atmospheric composition (CO_2 and N). Numerous authors contribute to the discussion of global impacts caused by invasive species including Carla D'Antonio, Richard Mack, and Erika Zavaleta whose work has been treated elsewhere in this reading list. The book divides the 17 chapters into Dimensions of the Problem, Social Impacts, and Regional Examples to explore broad issues. For example, Dukes discusses how rising levels of atmospheric CO_2 may enhance the invasive process, perhaps as it already has by permitting range expansion of exotic annuals that interact with fire in desert systems, or as it may affect nitrogen fixation in more mesic systems. Barrett considers the microevolutionary impacts global change may have as plants become exposed to herbicides, or "hybridize" with genotypes adapted to different environments. Two chapters examine the economic effects of invasive species; Zavaleta discusses the impacts of *Tamarix* invasions specifically. The regional examples from South Africa, Germany, New Zealand, and Chile offer management perspectives from areas at different stages of the invasive process. For example, New Zealand may still be able to eradicate some invasive species from some islands, and the Chile example suggests prioritizing based on the susceptibility of the system. Although this book does not treat individual species, plants alone, or specific problems, it puts the invasive species problem in perspective: a global perspective that managers can consider when pondering invasive species management in protected areas in the United States.

Office of Technology Assessment (OTA), U.S. Congress. 1993. Harmful nonindigenous species in the United States. Washington, DC: U.S. Government Printing Office; OTA F 565. 390 p.

Annotation: The OTA reviews the status, consequences, and introduction pathways of harmful nonindigenous species (NIS) in the United States, along with Federal and State legislation affecting their management. They conclude that: (1) the increasing number and negative impacts of harmful NIS "are creating a growing ecological and economic burden for the country;" (2) current policies are inadequate to address the growing problem of harmful NIS; and (3) a national policy is needed to more effectively screen harmful introduced species and to provide funding for rapid, coordinated responses to new threats. Natural areas in particular require greater protection from NIS. The authors review Federal policy toward NIS and make specific recommendations for important policy changes. They also discuss decisionmaking processes and technologies for preventing and managing NIS problems. This report is recommended for those interested in policy issues and management strategies for invasive species.

Olson, Bret E. 1999a. Impacts of noxious weeds on ecologic and economic systems. In: Sheley, Roger L.; Petroff, Janet K., eds. Biology and management of noxious rangeland weeds. Corvallis, OR: Oregon State University Press: 4 18.

Annotation: This chapter provides an overview of the effects of noxious weeds on species assemblages, ecosystem processes, and rangeland economics. Noxious weeds affect the diversity and relative abundance of both plant and animal species, alter vegetation physiognomy and soil structure, and modify ecosystem processes such as nutrient cycling, hydrology, temperature regimes, and fire return intervals. The ecological and economic value of range and agricultural lands generally decrease, and management costs increase, when noxious weeds invade. As invasive species continue to spread, their potential to impact economics at a regional scale also increases.

Pieterse, Arnold H.; Murphy, Kevin J., eds. 1990. Aquatic weeds: the ecology and management of nuisance aquatic vegetation. Oxford, UK: Oxford University Press. 593 p.

Annotation: See section III.E.1. Page 43.

Pimentel, David; Lach, Lori; Zuniga, Rodolfo; Morrison, Doug. 2000. Environmental and economic costs of nonindigenous species in the United States. Bioscience. 50: 53 65.

Annotation: Pimentel and others quantified the economic costs associated with nonindigenous species in the United States. Nonindigenous species were divided into eight distinct categories: plants, mammals, birds, reptiles and amphibians, fishes, arthropods, mollusks, and microbes. Their assessment on plants estimated that 5,000 nonnative plant species exist in natural ecosystems within the United States and that invasive plants cost the country over $7.5 billion annually in losses, damages, and control expenditures. They also discussed the effect of various nonindigenous species on native biota, both environmentally and economically. The authors projected a much higher economic impact ($137 billion annually) from nonindigenous species than did the Office of Technology Assessment (OTA) ($1.1 billion annually). The vast difference in estimates was derived from the authors' inclusion of more than 10 times the number of species that the OTA reported, and differing cost analyses.

Randall, John M. 1997. Defining weeds of natural areas. In: Luken, James O.; Thieret, John W., eds. Assessment and management of plant invasions. New York, NY: Springer Verlag: 18 25.

Annotation: This paper examines multiple definitions of "weeds," then defines and provides examples of natural area weeds. Randall emphasizes that natural area managers should clearly articulate what they are managing for before attempting to determine which species interfere with management goals and therefore are considered "weeds." He briefly outlines an adaptive management strategy for natural area weeds: (1) establishing management goals, (2) developing and implementing control programs based on these goals, (3) monitoring and assessing the impacts of control efforts, and (4) modifying goals and control programs as needed.

Richardson, David M.; Pysek, Petr; Rejmánek, Marcel; Barbour, Michael G.; Panetta, F. Dane; West, Carol J. 2000. Naturalization and invasion of alien plants: concepts and definitions. Diversity and Distributions. 6: 93 107.

Annotation: An examination of the term "naturalized" in dictionaries, ecological encyclopedias, books about invasions, and 157 publications revealed widespread and varied use of the term. After presenting four common definitions of the term, introducing potential reasons for this inconsistency, and explaining problems that result from it, the authors propose a standard set of definitions for the following terms: introduction, naturalized, invasion, weed, and transformer species. The first three terms are explained in terms of overcoming barriers to their spread (in other words, geographic, environmental at the site of introduction, reproductive, dispersal, environmental in disturbed habitats, and environmental in natural habitats). Introduction refers to species that have crossed a geographic barrier. Naturalized species overcome initial environmental and reproductive barriers, and naturalized populations are sustained over multiple life cycles without human intervention; however, these species are not necessarily invasive. The term invasion is reserved for naturalized plants that disperse and reproduce away from the sites of introduction, and successfully overcome environmental barriers in their new

locations. Additionally, the authors recommend reserving the term invasive for alien species, and referring to local vegetation succession (for example, shrub "invasion" of grassland) as colonization or encroachment. While the U.S. Presidential Executive Order (1999) and the IUCN (1999) refer to "invasive" species as alien species that cause ecological or economic impact, the authors suggest that the term invasion should not connote impact. Rather, they recommend referring to harmful alien and native species as weeds. Finally, transformer species are invasive species that "change the character, condition, form or nature of ecosystems," such as those that excessively use resources, donate resources, or alter fire regimes.

Stapanian, Martin A.; Sundberg, Scott D.; Baumgardner, Greg A.; Liston, Aaron. 1998. Alien plant species composition and associations with anthropogenic disturbance in North American forests. Plant Ecology. 139: 49 62.

Annotation: The authors compared alien plant diversity, cover, and origin among 279 forest plots in seven forested regions of the United States. See full annotation in section II.B.2. Page 21.

Vitousek, Peter M.; D'Antonio, Carla M.; Loope, Lloyd L.; Westbrooks, Randy. 1996. Biological invasions as global environmental change. American Scientist. 84: 468 478.

Annotation: This popular article describes the geographic extent and ecological impacts of invasive species at a global scale. In it, the authors outline the consequences of biological invasions to humans and the environment. Invasive species can act as vectors of human, livestock, and crop diseases, cause regional and national economic losses, permanently alter ecosystems, and reduce biological diversity. Moreover, different invasive species can act in tandem to exacerbate these problems. The authors conclude that greater awareness, legislative improvements, and collective action to eliminate invasive species are essential for preserving our economies and ecosystems.

Westbrooks, Randy G. 1998. Invasive plants, changing the landscape of America: fact book. Washington, DC: Federal Interagency Committee for the Management of Noxious and Exotic Weeds. 107 p. (Note: This book can be accessed online at *http://www.denix.osd.mil/denix/Public/ES Programs/Conservation/Invasive/intro.html*.)

Annotation: This informative, well illustrated publication resulted from an interagency effort to educate the public about North America's invasive weed problem. The first half is devoted to discussing the wide ranging threat posed by invasive plants, the history of introductions, their economic and ecological impacts, and the role of Federal, State, and local governments in managing them. Following is a section on the status and impacts of invasive plants in agricultural and rangelands, yards and gardens, forests, deserts, and wetlands. Special sections discuss the status, impacts, and management of invasive plants in Hawaii and Florida as well as in various parks, preserves, and recreation areas. The book contains illustrated "primers" that discuss the history, status, and management of invasive plant species deemed the most important in North America by the Federal Interagency Committee for the Management of Noxious and Exotic Weeds. Examples include purple nutsedge, kudzu, tamarisk, melaleuca, yellow star thistle, purple loosestrife, and cheatgrass.

B. Understanding Plant Invasions

A major focus of invasive plant research has been identify ing and assessing the relative importance of various factors that promote plant invasions. Despite such research, the abil ity to predict which introduced species will invade a given ecosystem remains poor. The following papers provide back ground on the theory and research behind how and why plant invasions occur. These papers discuss which biological at tributes of plants make them successful invaders as well as which environmental features make communities more or less vulnerable to invasion. Specifically, these works discuss fac tors that either increase or decrease the probability of inva sions, including life history strategies (Bazzaz 1986), genetic variability of introduced populations (Barrett 1992), the role of native plant diversity and resource availability (Stohlgren and others 1998, 1999a, 1999b, Levine and D'Antonio 1999), and the role of disturbance (Cadenasso and Pickett 2001, Hobbs and Huenneke 1992).

Disturbances (for example, fire, floods, erosion, grazing) play a central role in most plant invasions. Although some species invade relatively undisturbed habitats, many invasive plants preferentially colonize areas immediately following some form of disturbance. In general, disturbance facilitates plant invasions by temporarily eliminating competition from native species and by increasing the availability of nutrients. Hobbs (1989, 1991) and Hobbs and Huenneke (1992) provide broad overviews of the role of disturbance in promoting plant invasions. Stapanian and others (1998) and Stohlgren and oth ers (1999b) discuss the role of disturbance in forest habitats and Rocky Mountain grasslands, respectively. Stohlgren and others (1998) also discuss how flood related disturbance pro motes the establishment of early successional invaders in oth erwise diverse riparian areas. Davis and others (2000) ultimately explain disturbance, along with other theories of community invasibility, in terms of fluctuating resource avail ability.

1. Biological Characteristics of Invading Species

Allendorf, Fred W.; Holt, Jodie S.; Lodge, David M.; Molofsky, Jane; With, Kimberly A.; Baughman, Syndallas; Cabin, Robert J.; Cohen, Joel E.; Ellstrand, Norman C.; McCauley, David E.; O'Neil, Pamela; Parker, Ingrid M.; Thompson, John N.; Weller, Stephen G. 2001. The popu lation biology of invasive species. Annual Review of Ecol ogy and Systematics. 32: 305 332.

Annotation: Understanding the population biology of inva sive species may provide valuable insight for managing these species. Characteristics that allow initial colonization may differ from those that permit successful establishment or com petitive or dispersal ability. Population biologists can help guide management decisions by examining the genetic and evolutionary theory behind the invasion process. The authors summarize current knowledge of how genetic processes may affect a species potential to colonize a new area, the lag time between colonization and spread, and the range expansion of species. Moreover, population biology can address the invasibility of communities (for example, by studying the ef fects of habitat fragmentation and isolation on range expan sion), especially as management strives to restore invaded communities. Excellent opportunities exist for integrating research and management, and the authors encourage devel oping relationships between academic and management com munities.

Ashton, Peter. J.; Mitchell, David. S. 1989. Aquatic plants: patterns and modes of invasion, attributes of invading spe cies and assessment of control programmes. In: Drake, J. A.; Mooney, H. A.; di Castri, F.; Groves, R. H.; Kruger, F. J.; Rejmánek, M.; Williamson, M., eds. Biological invasions: a global perspective. Chichester, England: John Wiley and Sons: 111 154.

Annotation: Invasive aquatic plants are a major problem in freshwater habitats around the world. The authors thoroughly review the processes of dispersal, establishment, and invasion in freshwater aquatic plants. Dispersal of propagules is a criti cal element of the invasion process that has been greatly aided by humans, either by direct transport or by engineering projects that disturb or modify freshwater flows. Species most likely to become established in a new region are those that have multiple reproductive strategies, alternative morphologies that are more adaptive under different environmental conditions (in other words, phenotypic plasticity), vegetative (in other words, asexual) reproduction, and high growth rates. The po tential for a plant to invade is specific to the invading species and to the environment in which it is introduced. In general though, invaders are more likely to succeed if they originate from a similar environment, are able to survive periods of des iccation or siltation, lack competitors, parasites, and herbi vores in the new environment, or benefit from disturbance. The six main strategies for controlling invasive aquatic plants include: (1) manual removal, (2) mechanical removal, (3) chemical control, (4) biological control, (5) environmental manipulation (such as reservoir drawdown), and (6) harvest ing for other uses. The authors discuss the advantages and disadvantages of each approach. Overall, they suggest that rapid identification and eradication is the best approach, based on a plan of integrated control, followup monitoring, and backup control measures. Improved legislation and restrictions on the current trade in known invasive plants by the aquacul ture industry are vital for preventing future invasions.

Barrett, Spencer C. H. 1992. Genetics of weed invasions. In: Jain, S. K.; Botsford, L. W., eds. Applied population biol ogy. Dordrecht, The Netherlands: Kluwer Academic Publish ers: 91 119.

Annotation: The genetic makeup of an introduced plant popu lation is now recognized as an important factor contributing to its success or failure at becoming an invader. In this paper, the authors use case studies of two globally important inva sive plants, water hyacinth and barnyard grass, to review how genetic factors influence a plant's invasive ability. The level of genetic variation in an introduced population has important consequences for invasive ability. Populations with high lev els of genetic variation generally are better able to respond to natural selection in a new environment, thereby facilitating their establishment and spread. Such populations may also be better able to withstand biocontrol efforts or develop resis tance to specialized herbicides. Genetic markers can be used to identify the geographic origin of specific populations of invasive plants. This may ultimately aid in efforts to obtain effective biocontrol agents from within the native range of the plant. Factors contributing to increased genetic variability in introduced populations include multiple introductions from different sources, outcrossing, hybridization with closely re lated native taxa, and sexual recombination (rather than self fertilization or asexual budding). Introduced populations that arise from single introductions and those that exhibit asexual reproduction tend to have low genetic variability and are the easiest to control.

Bazzaz, F. A. 1986. Life history of colonizing plants: some demographic, genetic, and physiological features. In: Mooney, Harold A.; Drake, James A., eds. Ecology of bio logical invasions of North America and Hawaii. New York, NY: Springer Verlag: 96 110.

Annotation: Plants may have special life history features that enable them to colonize or invade new habitats. The author reviews a number of key demographic, genetic, and physi ological features of such plants, including their dispersal ca pability, genetic diversity as a result of their breeding system (in other words, self pollination and outcrossing), level of "preadaptation" (in other words, compatibility) in their new environment, physiology, and competitive overlap with na tive species. He concludes that efficient dispersal, preadap tations, larger numbers of initial propagules, and the ability of growing plants to respond to different environments by de veloping different morphologies or life history traits (phenotypic plasticity) are key elements of successful colonization.

Burke, M. J. W.; Grime, J. P. 1996. An experimental study of plant community invasibility. Ecology. 77(3): 776 790.

Annotation: See section II.B.2. Page 15.

Callaway, Ragan M.; Aschehoug, Erik T. 2000. Invasive plants versus their new and old neighbors: a mechanism for exotic invasion. Science. 290: 521 523.

Annotation: Invasive plants generally are thought to succeed because they are no longer held in check by natural predators or parasites. However, in this paper, the authors experimen tally demonstrate that knapweed (*Centaurea diffusa*), an in vasive plant in Western North America, produces toxic chemicals (in other words, allelopathy) whose inhibitory ef fects are greater on North American grasses than on grasses with which it evolved in Asia. This suggests that plant com munities evolve defenses against allelopathy over time, and that allelopathy may allow invading species to compete more successfully in new environments.

Reichard, Sarah Hayden; Hamilton, Clement W. 1997. Predicting invasions of woody plants introduced into North America. Conservation Biology. 11(1): 193 203.

Annotation: See section III.C. Page 38.

Rejmánek, Marcel. 1996. A theory of seed plant invasive ness: the first sketch. Biological Conservation. 78: 171 181.

Annotation: The author ties together four disparate lines of evidence to create a general model for predicting invasiveness of seed plants: (1) historical data on taxonomic differences between invaders and natives, (2) life history characteris tics of invasive and noninvasive pines, (3) data on the ex tent of native geographic ranges of grasses and composites, and (4) new information on the effect of genome size (the number of chromosomes it has) on invasive ability. Fac tors that promote invasiveness include low seed mass, short juvenile period, short interval between large seed crops,

vegetative (asexual) reproduction, small genome size, a distant taxonomic relationship to native species, seed dis persal by vertebrates, and high habitat compatibility. The author also recommends several promising avenues of re search, including examining the relationship of various genetic characters to invasive potential and researching unexplained time lags between introductions and subsequent invasions.

Rejmánek, Marcel; Richardson, David M. 1996. What at tributes make some plant species more invasive? Ecology. 77(6): 1655 1661.

Annotation: This paper shows that a small number of bio logical characteristics can successfully predict the invasibility of pines. The authors used a discriminant analy sis to identify characteristics of 24 species of invasive and noninvasive pines found around the world. Only three of 10 life history characters included in the initial analysis were needed to maximize the difference between the two groups: mean seed mass, minimum juvenile period, and mean interval between large seed crops. Based on these three characteristics, the discriminant function correctly classified 38 of 40 species of woody seed plants as either invasive or noninvasive. Two species were incorrectly clas sified as noninvasive because the model did not account for seed dispersal by vertebrates. In combination, the dis criminant function equation, seed mass values, and the op portunity for seed dispersal by vertebrates provide a useful and reliable method for predicting the invasibility of pines and other woody seed plants.

Richardson, D. M.; Williams, P. A.; Hobbs, R. J. 1994. Pine invasions in the Southern Hemisphere: determi nants of spread and invadability. Journal of Biogeogra phy. 21: 511 527.

Annotation: In reviewing the ecology of pine (*Pinus* spp.) invasions in the Southern Hemisphere, several general pat terns were evident: (1) pines with mechanisms for long dis tance seed dispersal (wind or animal mediated) colonize and persist in habitats that experience regular disturbance; (2) resi dence time since introduction is positively correlated with the geographic extent of invasion; and (3) forests, shrublands, grasslands, dunes and bare ground, in that or der, were increasingly susceptible to pine invasions. None theless, certain dominant species of understory plants tended to prohibit pine invasions, while the extent and severity of disturbance (either natural or human induced) appeared to be one of the primary factors promoting the spread and persistence of invasive pines.

Woods, Kerry D. 1997. Community response to plant in vasion. In: Luken, James O.; Thieret, John W., eds. Assess ment and Management of Plant Invasions. New York, NY: Springer Verlag: 56 68.

Annotation: See section II.C.1. Page 28.

2. Site Characteristics and Disturbance History

Baker, H. G. 1986. Patterns of plant invasion in North America. In: Mooney, Harold A.; Drake, James A., eds. Ecol ogy of biological invasions of North America and Hawaii. New York, NY: Springer Verlag: 44 57.

Annotation: See section II.A. Page 9.

Bossard, C. C. 1991. The role of habitat disturbance, seed predation and ant dispersal on establishment of the exotic shrub *Cytisus scoparius* in California. American Midland Naturalist. 126(1): 1 13.

Annotation: This study assessed the effects of vegetation and soil disturbance on seedling establishment of scotch broom (*Cytisus scoparius*) at two California locations with different climatic and edaphic conditions (a foothill and a coastal site), and it sought to assess the interaction of this disturbance with animal dispersers and prey. Results, consistent with other stud ies, showed that soil disturbance increased scotch broom ger mination and establishment at the foothill site. This was not the case at the coastal site, and this difference was due to the foraging activities of quail and grouse. The soil disturbance conditions that enhanced scotch broom establishment and growth at the foothill site also enhanced predation at the coastal site, decreasing establishment. These results suggest that a variety of interactions may occur within disturbed areas over time, biotic factors can have a larger impact than abiotic fac tors, and the effects of disturbance on invasive establishment can not be generalized from one population or habitat to another.

Brandt, C. A.; Rickard, W. H. 1994. Alien taxa in the North American shrub-steppe four decades after cessation of live- stock grazing and cultivation of agriculture. Biological Con servation. 68(2): 95 106.

Annotation: The authors document the status of nonnative plants and animals on the Columbia River Plain in central Washington. The Columbia River Plain is one of the largest and most important areas of remaining native, shrub steppe habitat. Although the plain has acted as a de facto nature pre serve since the mid 1940s, nonnative plants are nonetheless widespread and have a significant negative effect on native wildlife. Six invasive plant species were abundant across plots, with cheatgrass (*Bromus tectorum*) being the most widespread and ecologically important. It occurred in both disturbed and undisturbed areas, readily invaded burned areas, promoted more frequent burns, and appeared to have the greatest nega tive impacts on both native plant and animal communities.

Briese, D. T. 1996. Biological control of weeds and fire management in protected nature areas: are they compat- ible strategies? Biological Conservation. 77(2 3): 135 141.

Annotation: A complex interaction exists among fire, weeds, and a biological control agent in a natural area in Australia. Prescribed fire, a common management practice in Australia, led to increases in a population of St. Johnswort (*Hypericum perforatum*) in both open and forested areas. At the same time, these fires suppressed populations of St. Johnswort's princi pal biological control agent. Ultimately populations of the biocontrol were able to rebound in response to increased plant nutrient levels, which, in turn, were a response to the fire. Effects of fire on weeds and biocontrol agents may vary de pending on the scale, intensity, frequency of occurrence, and seasonal timing of the fire regime. The author recommends that interactions among fire, weeds, and biocontrol agents be considered and that managers work to make fire and weed management compatible in protected natural areas.

Brooks, Matthew L.; Pyke, David A. 2001. Invasive plants and fire in the deserts of North America. In: Galley, Krista E. M.; Wilson, Tyrone P., eds. Proceedings of the invasive species workshop: the role of fire in the control and spread of invasive species. Fire Conference 2000: The First National Congress on Fire Ecology, Prevention, and Management. Misc. Pub. No. 11, Tall Timbers Research Station, Tallahassee, FL: 1 14.

Annotation: See section II.C.1. Page 24.

Brothers, Timothy S.; Spingarn, Arthur. 1992. Forest frag- mentation and alien plant invasion of central Indiana old- growth forests. Conservation Biology. 6(1): 91 100.

Annotation: Old growth forest fragments in Indiana appeared to be relatively resistant to invasion: exotic species richness and frequency within forests decreased significantly with in creasing distance toward the interior from forest edges. In addition, with the exception of a few shade tolerant aliens, forest interiors were relatively free of exotics. Invasions may be limited by low light availability in forest interiors, limited dispersal ability, low levels of disturbance, or by forest edges. Forest edges typically consist of a dense wall of bordering vegetation that reduces light and wind speed and may limit dispersal of invasive plants. Despite the apparent resistance of these mesic old growth forest fragments to invasion, the authors caution that future introductions of shade tolerant spe cies remain a threat.

Burke, M. J. W.; Grime, J. P. 1996. An experimental study of plant community invasibility. Ecology. 77(3): 776 790.

Annotation: Most previous studies of invasibility have fo cused on identifying characteristics of successful invaders or features of plant communities that make them susceptible to invasion. In this study, the authors experimentally tested how the size of gaps in existing vegetation, level of disturbance, and soil fertility affect the establishment and spread of weeds. Levels of disturbance and soil fertility were the most impor tant predictors of invasibility, with the highest rates of inva sion in the most disturbed, most heavily fertilized plots. Although disturbance may allow individuals of the invasive species to colonize an area, variation in soil nutrient levels are what determine the invader's growth rate after germination and therefore its ability to become established in the face of future disturbance and/or competition from natives. Large seed size, a character normally thought to reduce a plant's invasive ability, appeared instead to promote germination and persis tence, regardless of the level of disturbance or fertilization. The authors conclude that predicting a plant's invasive poten tial involves considering not only the affected area's soil fer tility, disturbance regime, and the distribution of gaps within the habitat, but also the life history characteristics of the po tential invader.

Burns, Charmion; Sauer, Jonathan. 1992. Resistance by natural vegetation in the San Gabriel Mountains of Cali- fornia to invasions by introduced conifers. Global Ecology and Biogeography Letters. 2: 46 51.

Annotation: This paper is unusual in the literature in that it documents the complete failure of more than 45 introduced conifer species to invade the chaparral or pine oak woodlands of the San Gabriel Mountains in southern California. Although several species have become established in restricted locations, none have become invasive. The authors attribute this pattern to the lack of nutrient rich soils, the presence of a severe physical environment, especially drought and frequent, severe fires, and the existence of dense and diverse native vegetation.

Cadenasso, M. L.; Pickett, S. T. A. 2001. Effect of edge structure on the flux of species into forest interiors. Con servation Biology. 15(1): 91 97.

Annotation: This research assessed the importance of the for est edge to weed invasion from the surrounding landscape. The researchers used an experimental, spatially explicit ap proach and directly measured wind dispersed seed flux into a deciduous forest patch in New York, comparing sections of the forest edge that were thinned (simulating logging) to unal tered sections. Significantly more seeds entered the forest in terior of the thinned treatment relative to the unaltered treatment. The intact edge functioned as a physical barrier to wind dispersed seeds, even after autumn leaf drop. These re sults counter assumptions that "everything can get everywhere" and show that dispersal may be a limiting factor for invaders. In addition to the oft made recommendation to reduce the ra tio of edge to interior, managers may want to consider the structure of the forest edge vegetation. Sealing the edge of the disturbance or the wilderness boundary with native vegeta tion may prevent the spread of invasives into the forest or pro tected area.

Crawley, Michael J. 1987. What makes a community invasible? In: Gray, A. J.; Crawley, M. J.; Edwards, P. J., eds. Colonization, succession and stability. Oxford, England: Blackwell Scientific Publications: 429 453.

Annotation: Determining which biotic communities are invasible is a critical question in invasive plant ecology. After reviewing introduced plant records in the British Isles, the author concluded that all biological communities are invasible to varying degrees, but that the presence of bare ground, in creased levels of disturbance, and proximity to dispersal path ways (for example, roads, ports, cities) tend to promote exotic plant invasions. The author also examined insect species in troduced as biocontrols in Britain to determine which were most likely to become established and why. Insects that were abundant and had large geographic ranges in their native re gion were most likely to spread after introduction, while un predictable events (such as bad weather, predation by ants) played a large role in failed introductions. In general, those insect species most likely to invade and those communities most likely to be invaded could not accurately be predicted.

Davis, Mark A.; Grime, J. Philip; Thompson, Ken. 2000. Fluctuating resources in plant communities: a general theory of invasibility. Journal of Ecology. 88: 528 534.

Annotation: The likelihood of invasions occurring depends on three factors: availability of invading propagules, biologi cal characteristics of the invading species, and community invasibility. The authors demonstrate that most theories of com munity invasibility can be explained by a single theory of fluc tuating resource availability, which is based on the assumption that invading species need accessible resources to become established. This theory integrates hypotheses of disturbance, competition, herbivory, mutualism, and facilitation. For ex ample, disturbance enhances invasibility by removing veg etation or cover, which makes additional resources available. In addition to reduced use of resources, gross resource avail ability can increase (for example, due to climate changes). Previous theories characterize invasibility as an inherent

attribute of communities, whereas this theory suggests the invasibility of a community can change over time as the amount of unused resources fluctuates. The authors demonstrate sup port for this theory by reviewing a variety of studies; they also provide testable predictions for future investigations.

Dudley, T.; Embury, M. 1995. Nonindigenous species in wilderness areas: the status and impacts of livestock and game species in designated wilderness in California. Oak land, CA: Pacific Institute for Studies in Development, Envi ronment, and Security. 38 p.

Annotation: See section I. Page 6.

Floyd-Hanna, Lisa; Romme, William; Kendall, Deborah; Loy, Allan; Colyer, Marilyn. 1993. Succession and biologi cal invasion at Mesa Verde NP. Park Science. Fall: 16 18.

Annotation: The authors showed that nonnative musk thistles invaded burned areas after fire in Mesa Verde National Park. While natural disturbance factors are essential to maintaining many community and ecosystem processes, they can also pro mote habitat degradation and invasion by exotics. Parts of the park that have experienced human related disturbances, such as road and waterline construction, sewage facilities, and live stock grazing, are also particularly prone to invasion. The au thors used two thistle species to illustrate the extent of nonnative invasions into the park and discuss possible man agement strategies to control them.

Forcella, Frank; Harvey, Stephen J. 1983. Eurasian weed infestation in western Montana in relation to vegetation and disturbance. Madroño. 30(2): 102 109.

Annotation: Paired surveys were conducted to compare road side infestations of exotic weeds between disturbed roadside areas and areas away from roadsides with different levels of disturbance (for example, grazed or clearcut plots). The de gree of disturbance and time since disturbance were not ex plicitly considered. Even with relatively little disturbance, infestations were found in low montane forest (*Pinus ponde rosa*) and dry grassland steppe (*Bouteloua/Stipa*). In areas of intensive disturbance, infestations were primarily found at low to mid elevations, but extended up into mid montane Dou glas fir (*Pseudotsuga menziesii*) forests. Regardless of the level of disturbance, the higher elevation subalpine zone did not have weed infestations. The authors suggest several possible explanations for these patterns (for example, radiation levels and climate).

Galley, Krista E. M.; Wilson, Tyrone P. 2001. Proceedings of the invasive species workshop: the role of fire in the control and spread of invasive species. Fire Conference 2000: The First National Congress on Fire Ecology, Prevention, and Management. Misc. Pub. No. 11, Tall Timbers Research Sta tion, Tallahassee, FL. 147 p.

Annotation: This invasive species workshop was developed based on the Joint Fire Services Governing Board's white pa per that identified the need for scientific perspectives related to fire management practices and invasive species. The work shop was designed to bring together the state of knowledge about the interactions between fire and invasive species, to identify management needs, and to raise public awareness about fire/invasive species issues. Although weeds are prima rily considered a problem in Western States, the workshop was focused nationally. The workshop proceedings are divided into major eco regions including desert/semidesert environments, temperate grasslands, Mediterranean climates, temperate and boreal coniferous forests, temperate deciduous forests, and tropical and subtropical environments.

Grace, James B.; Smith, Melinda D.; Grace, Susan L.; Collins, Scott L.; Stohlgren, Thomas J. 2001. Interactions between fire and invasive plants in temperate grasslands of North America. In: Galley, Krista E. M.; Wilson, Tyrone P., eds. Proceedings of the invasive species workshop: the role of fire in the control and spread of invasive species. Fire Con ference 2000: The First National Congress on Fire Ecology, Prevention, and Management. Misc. Pub. No. 11, Tall Tim bers Research Station, Tallahassee, FL: 40 65.

Annotation: The authors list 24 grass species, 25 forbs, and eight woody species considered to be of major concern as in vaders of grassland ecosystem in North America. For the most egregious of these species, they describe what little is known about their interactions with fire. Each of these species re sponds differently to fire. Many species alter natural fire re gimes either by enhancing fuel loads (for example, cheatgrass [*Bromus tectorum*] and saltcedar [*Tamarix* spp.]) or by reduc ing the ability of fire to spread (for example, Chinese tallow [*Triadica sebifera*], leafy spurge [*Euphorbia esula*], and spot ted knapweed [*Centaurea biebersteinii* {= *C. maculosa*}]). Based on a conceptual framework model they developed, the authors present a table for 20 of these invasive species. The table addresses questions about how these invasives relate to fire, including the following: (1) does fire enhance coloniza tion, (2) how does fire affect the invasive species' survival, (3) do invasive plants recover after fire and how quickly, (4) is competition with native species important, and (5) how do invasive species affect the historic fire regime? While no man agement panacea is available, the authors develop models to describe seven patterns of invasive species interactions with fire and the native community, and provide examples that il lustrate how invasive species affect specific grassland com munities and landscapes. The authors suggest managers use fire as part of a multifaceted approach to invasive weed man agement, including the consideration of climate, habitat, and growing conditions for each invasive species. Species that al ter the fire regime may require intensive human intervention.

Greenberg, Cathryn H.; Crownover, Stanley H.; Gordon, Doria R. 1997. Roadside soils: a corridor for invasion of xeric scrub by nonindigenous plants. Natural Areas Jour nal. 17(2): 99 109.

Annotation: This study tested the hypothesis that modified soils (limerock and clay) used in constructing roads through sand pine scrub habitat in Florida provide a suitable corridor for invasions of nonindigenous species and native species that do not normally occur in dry scrub (uncharacteristic species). The percent cover and species richness of uncharacteristic and exotic species were significantly lower in sandy areas and clearcuts, despite soil disturbances, than in areas with intro duced clay and limerock soils. The percent cover and species richness of native species was significantly higher in sandy areas and clearcuts. The low level of exotic and uncharacter istic species along roads with sand edges and in clearcuts sug gest that xeric scrub habitat is resistant to invasion, even in the face of disturbance, as long as native soils are present. In contrast, the presence of clay and limerock soils along roads appeared to facilitate the invasion and establishment of

uncharacteristic and exotic species. Land managers should exercise caution when deciding on if, where, and with which types of soils roads are constructed in natural areas.

Hester, A. J.; Hobbs, R. J. 1992. Influence of fire and soil nutrients on native and nonnative annuals at remnant veg etation edges in the Western Australia wheatbelt. Journal of Vegetation Science. 3: 101 108.

Annotation: This study examined the effect of fire and soil nutrients on native and nonnative annual plants in shrubland and woodland fragments in western Australia. Density and cover of exotic plants were highest at fragment edges and de creased toward the interior. Fewer nonnative plants were found in either burned or unburned shrubland than in woodland. Fire did not facilitate the invasion of exotics in either habitat. Soil phosphorus levels were strongly correlated with the abundance of exotic plants only in unburned shrubland. Postfire increases in nutrients did not lead to increased colonization by exotics, suggesting that nutrient increases alone are not sufficient to allow invasion in these two particular kinds of communities. This study also examined the impact of removal of exotic an nuals on native annuals. The removal of exotic plants led to a significant increase in the percent cover of native plants. Smaller suppressed native species showed dramatic increases in growth, presumably in response to decreased competition. Two native species also showed increased seed production. Removal of native plants had no effect on the total cover of exotic plants.

Hobbs, Richard J. 1989. The nature and effects of distur bance relative to invasions. In: Drake, J. A.; Mooney, H. A.; di Castri, F.; Groves, R. H.; Kruger, F. J.; Rejmánek, M.; Williamson, M., eds. Biological invasions: a global perspec tive. Chichester, England: John Wiley and Sons: 389 401.

Annotation: This study compared the relative invasibility of undisturbed plots to that of disturbed plots, both with and with out added fertilizers, in five Australian habitats. The author examined how physical and/or chemical disturbances influ enced invasions by exotic annual plants. Nonnative plants re sponded most to the combination of disturbance and the addition of fertilizer. Windblown additions of nutrients into natural areas experiencing natural disturbances are likely to lead to increased invasions by exotic annual plants. Wood land communities were the most susceptible to invasion whereas heath was the most resistant habitat type. The author concludes with a discussion of various types of disturbances and their potential effects on communities, and speculates that the particular attributes of a system (for example, which re sources are limiting or the nature of disturbance regimes) will determine whether and how disturbance influences invasibility.

Hobbs, Richard J. 1991. Disturbance a precursor to weed invasion in native vegetation. Plant Protection Quarterly. 6(3): 99 104.

Annotation: This paper focuses on the potential link between disturbance and invasion by exotic plants. The author first explores various definitions of disturbance and examines the extent to which weed invasions are dependent on disturbance in Australia. Hobbs then presents the findings of studies that examined the effects of different types of disturbance (for ex ample, fire, nutrient addition, edge effects, soil disturbance) on invasions in several types of ecosystems. The studies show that plant communities vary greatly in their susceptibility to invasion, that some, but not all, types of disturbance greatly increase the likelihood of invasion, and that invasion is most likely in communities subject to a combination of disturbances. Finally, Hobbs suggests several principles for managing disturbance including maintaining natural disturbance regimes, minimizing disturbance caused by human activities, and being aware of synergisms operating between different types of disturbance.

Hobbs, Richard J.; Huenneke, Laura F. 1992. Disturbance, diversity, and invasion: implications for conservation. Conservation Biology. 6(2): 324 337.

Annotation: Disturbance, a critical element of natural eco systems that helps maintain biotic diversity, may also promote invasions of nonnative plants by increasing the invasibility of communities. The authors discuss and provide examples of the types of disturbance important in maintaining plant species diversity and those that promote invasions. Focusing primarily on grasslands, they address fire, grazing, soil disturbances, nutrient inputs, trampling, fragmentation, and interactions among these types of disturbances. They conclude that it is often alterations to existing regimes and interactions between different disturbances that most often promote invasions. Natural disturbance regimes have now been disrupted in most areas of conservation concern, and fragmentation and anthropogenic changes have modified physical and biotic conditions. The authors therefore encourage managers to take an active role in implementing disturbance regimes that fit the landscape, the biotic community, and specific conservation goals.

Huenneke, Laura F.; Hamburg, Steven P.; Koide, Roger; Mooney, Harold A.; Vitousek, Peter M. 1990. Effects of soil resources on plant invasion and community structure in Californian serpentine grassland. Ecology. 71(2): 478 491.

Annotation: In contrast to many other studies, this research demonstrates that, even without physical disturbance of the soil or removal of native vegetation, increased nutrient avail ability can facilitate invasions of nonnative species. The authors examined the effect of increased nutrient availability on native and invasive nonnative plants in nutrient poor serpentine grasslands in California. Fertilization of study plots with nitrogen and phosphorus increased the biomass of the resident vegetation in the first season. Within 2 years, however, increased nutrient levels had allowed dominant exotic annual grasses to invade patches of native annual forbs. This has important implications for native vegetation in low nutrient habitats when deposition of atmospheric nitrogen is a problem.

Hughes, Flint; Vitousek, Peter M.; Tunison, Timothy. 1991. Alien grass invasion and fire in the seasonal submontane zone of Hawai'i. Ecology. 72(2): 743 746.

Annotation: To evaluate the relationship among invasive grasses, fire, and ecosystem attributes, the authors compared the species composition and vegetation structure of unburned plots against plots that had burned 18 years earlier, 15 months earlier, and those that burned on both occasions. Alien grass cover increased following fires, while native shrub and tree cover and diversity declined. Alien grasses persisted in the ecosystem after just one burn, and native shrub seedlings were unable to recolonize due to the dense cover of alien grasses following fires. Plots that burned twice were colonized by a second, more noxious weed, showing that successive fires can aggravate the impact of alien grasses on native vegetation. In addition to increasing fire intensity and decreasing the return interval, multiple invasions by increasingly detrimental alien grasses maintain the ecosystem in an altered state. This process converts long lived, diverse, native woodlands into grasslands dominated by highly flammable exotics.

Johnstone, I. M. 1986. Plant invasion windows: a time-based classification of invasive potential. Biological Review. 61: 369 394.

Annotation: After critically reviewing existing theoretical models of plant invasions, the author concludes that most apply only to specific ecological situations, and that only one, Harper's "safe sites" model, is generally applicable. Safe sites are defined as openings in time and space that allow invasive species to successfully germinate and become established. Based on that model, he suggests that invasions occur during "windows" when a barrier that previously excluded the invader from a community assemblage or site is removed. Johnstone then discusses the types of barriers that exist and the different kinds of invasion windows that occur.

Keeley, Jon E. 2001. Fire and invasive species in Mediterranean-climate ecosystems of California. In: Galley, Krista E. M.; Wilson, Tyrone P., eds. Proceedings of the invasive species workshop: the role of fire in the control and spread of invasive species. Fire Conference 2000: The First National Congress on Fire Ecology, Prevention, and Management. Misc. Pub. No. 11, Tall Timbers Research Station, Tallahassee, FL: 81 94.

Annotation: The Mediterranean climate region consists of the area west of the Great Basin, Mojave, and Colorado deserts from southern Oregon to northern Baja California. Over 4,400 plant species occur in the region, of which nearly half are endemic and one fourth are invasive species. Many of the invasive species were associated with disturbed landscapes in their historical range. As a result, nearly 60 percent of invasive plants are annuals associated with disturbed landscapes in California. Although the woody invasives also tend to be disturbance dependent, closed canopy shrublands and montane landscapes are relatively resistant to invasion. Fire may have been a factor allowing the type conversion from native perennial grasslands or shrublands to exotic annual grasslands even in fire dependent systems because plants evolve with a particular fire regime, not just with fire. In the chaparral system, the rate of invasion depends on the rate of postfire recovery by native shrubs, and the diversity of invasive species increases with increasing fire frequency. Moreover, these invasive annuals may increase fire frequency beyond what the native fire prone shrubs can tolerate. Therefore, in the Mediterranean climate ecosystem, management should consider the community being restored. In grassland communities, spring burning may increase the ratio of herbaceous perennials to invasive annuals, but fire will not restore native bunchgrasses in systems dominated by invasive plants. Fire is not recommended as a tool for restoration of California shrublands. In fact, fire suppression and prevention may be better management practices in these communities. In coniferous forests, fire restoration may promote invasion by nonnative species especially into gaps resulting from high fire intensity. Unfortunately, ponderosa pine (*Pinus ponderosa*) and giant sequoia (*Sequoiadendron giganteum*) depend upon gaps for new seedlings to become established. Therefore, although managing fires for low intensity may reduce the potential for invasion by nonnatives, eliminating seed sources of invasive species along roadsides and other disturbed sites may allow a more natural fire regime to be restored.

Levine, Jonathan M. 2000. Species diversity and biological invasions: relating local process to community pattern. Science. 288: 852 854.

Annotation: In spite of the classic hypothesis that diversity increases community resistance to invasions, communities containing diverse natural assemblages are often the most in vaded. To investigate this apparent contradiction, the author experimentally altered diversity in a natural setting of tussocks that comprised discrete island communities. Prior to manipu lation, he found a greater presence of exotic plants on more diverse tussocks. After he removed all species from the tus socks and replaced them with native species at varying levels of diversity, exotic plant establishment was lower on diverse tussocks. Thus, at the tussock scale, diversity appeared to en hance resistance to invasions. After conducting a second ex periment that indicated the intrinsic biotic and physical conditions of the tussocks were not driving the presence of exotic species in this ecosystem, he noted that invasion pat terns are likely due to factors that occur at greater scales than individual tussocks. For instance, changes in seed availability at broader scales can overwhelm the local effects of diversity. Citing the facts that tussock diversity was greater downstream and that seeds move downstream, he concludes that propagule supply, which covaries with diversity, is a more important fac tor in patterns of invasion seen in this ecosystem than local community diversity.

Levine, Jonathan M.; D'Antonio, Carla M. 1999. Elton revisited: a review of evidence linking diversity and invasibility. Oikos. 87: 15 26.

Annotation: These authors review, and ultimately challenge, the common assertion that low diversity promotes invasions. Invasibility is defined as the likelihood that new species be come established in communities. Many studies of the rela tionship between diversity and invasibility rely on classical niche theories based on the assumption that communities with low diversity have more available resources for invaders to exploit. While many of the theoretical studies reviewed sup ported a negative relationship between diversity and invasibility, empirical studies were mixed, and most spatial pattern studies supported a positive relationship. The authors agree with Stohlgren and others (1999) that the factors that control diversity are the same factors that control invasibility (for example, disturbance, resource availability, competition). Thus, investigating the mechanisms that control diversity, as well as those underlying positive or negative correlations be tween diversity and invisibility, may provide the most insight. Research is also needed to identify and understand species that facilitate invasions.

Lonsdale, W. M. 1999. Global patterns of plant invasions and the concept of invasibility. Ecology. 80(5): 1522 1536.

Annotation: Based on his analysis of 184 sites, Lonsdale finds that islands, on average, have more than twice as many exot ics as do mainland sites and that nonreserve sites have two times as many exotics as do reserves. Overall, almost 70 percent of the variation in the number of exotic species can be accounted for by three factors: the number of native species, whether the site is an island or on the mainland, and whether or not it is a nature reserve. The number of exotic species in nature reserves increases with the number of visitors. Com munities richer in native species have more exotics than do species poor communities. Temperate agricultural or urban sites are among the most invaded biomes, while desert and savannas are among the least. Finally, Lonsdale emphasizes the difficulty of drawing conclusions about relative invasibility, invasion potential, or the roles of dispersal and disturbance from any of these results.

Lyons, Kelly G.; Schwartz, Mark W. 2001. Rare species loss alters ecosystem function—invasion resistance. Ecol ogy Letters. 4: 358 365.

Annotation: Rather than compare differences in the initial diversity among communities, this study addressed the effect of changing diversity within communities. By experimentally removing rare native species from field plots and controlling for the resulting disturbance, the authors found that an intro duced exotic grass, *Lolium temulentum*, became more estab lished in plots where native species diversity had been successfully reduced. They explained that rare species might occupy niches with limited resources, such as water or nitro gen that more common species are unable to exploit. Allow ing rare species to disappear from a community may release these resources, thereby increasing community invasibility. In addition to highlighting the intrinsic value of rare species, these results support the conclusion that maintaining diversity may be a conservation priority in habitats that are threatened by invasive species.

Macdonald, I. A. W.; Frame, G. W. 1988. The invasion of introduced species into nature reserves in tropical savan nas and dry woodlands. Biological Conservation. 44: 67 93.

Annotation: See section I. Page 7.

Mack, Richard N. 1984. Invaders at home on the range. Natural History. 93(2): 40 47.

Annotation: This paper documents the historical spread of cheatgrass (*Bromus tectorum*) in the Intermountain West fol lowing agriculture and intensive cattle grazing. Mack first describes the evolution of the grasslands that comprise the Intermountain West. Grasslands on the Great Plains co evolved with large herds of bison. In contrast, grasslands of the Inter mountain region between the Cascade and Sierra Nevada ranges east to the Rocky Mountains evolved in the absence of large hoofed herbivores and therefore did not develop defenses against heavy grazing and trampling. The introduction of cattle to this area subjected the native grasslands to high levels of disturbance and facilitated the invasion of cheatgrass, an aggressive invader whose evolutionary history in Eurasia made it a highly suc cessful competitor on grazed and agricultural lands in the In termountain West. Mack also describes some of the adaptations that have made cheatgrass so successful in disturbed areas and describes its exponential spread on Western rangelands.

Mack, Richard N. 1989. Temperate grasslands vulnerable to plant invasions: characteristics and consequences. In: Drake, J. A.; Mooney, H. A.; di Castri, F.; Groves, R. H.; Kruger, F. J.; Rejmánek, M.; Williamson, M., eds. Biological invasions: a global perspective. Chichester, England: John Wiley and Sons: 155 179.

Annotation: The impact of invasive species has been espe cially severe in temperate grasslands. This article provides an excellent overview of factors promoting invasion in temper ate grasslands worldwide, the history of such invasions, and current threats to these ecosystems. The author argues that those temperate grasslands most susceptible to invasion have tussock grasses that evolved in the absence of persistent graz ing. These areas include the pampas of Argentina, the interior grasslands of Australia, California's Central Valley, and the U.S. Intermountain West. He then presents a historical per spective on plant invasions for each region. The accidental introduction of invasive plants via agriculture and ornamental horticulture as well as deliberate planting and seeding of po tential invasive plants (for example, *Kochia* spp.) for aesthetic reasons or erosion control continue to threaten temperate grass lands. The deliberate release of genetically engineered hybrids (for example, *Agropyron* spp.) could also have unanticipated adverse effects and should be reconsidered.

Milberg, Per; Lamont, Byron B. 1995. Fire enhances weed invasion of roadside vegetation in southwestern Australia. Biological Conservation. 73: 45 49.

Annotation: Remnant patches of roadside vegetation were invaded by nonnative species after fire. The authors compared changes in the number and percent cover of weeds in burned and unburned plots over a 7 year period. Weeds increased sig nificantly in the burned plots immediately after the fire, while native species declined. The impact of the fires was still evi dent 7 years after the study plots were burned, with weeds being significantly more abundant in the burned plots than in the little changed unburned control plots.

Orians, G. H. 1986. Site characteristics favoring invasions. In: Mooney, Harold A.; Drake, James A., eds. Ecology of bio logical invasions of North America and Hawaii. New York, NY: Springer Verlag: 133 148.

Annotation: This chapter discusses new avenues for thinking about and researching the dynamics between colonizing (in vading) species and colonized sites. The author points out that most previous research on this topic has either focused on characteristics of either invaders or of sites, or it has been con ducted at spatial and temporal scales inappropriate for the spe cies being studied. The suitability of an area for colonization by an introduced species depends on how well it meets the specific needs of the organism in question. Orians presents new ideas about how disturbance, in the form of changes in predation patterns and increases in resource availability, or trophic interactions, particularly species' chemical ecology, may affect suitability of an area from the perspective of plant, insect, or bird colonizers. It is also important to view inva sions at the scale of the generation time of the invading and affected organisms. Overall, this chapter reinforces the need to examine invasions on a case by case basis at the appropri ate scale rather than trying to make sweeping generalizations that invariably cannot apply to all biological systems.

Pyle, Laura L. 1995. Effects of disturbance on herbaceous exotic plant species on the floodplain of the Potomac River. American Midland Naturalist. 134(2): 244 253.

Annotation: Different types of disturbance can affect the invasibility of exotic plants differently. This study examined the extent to which human disturbance, in the form of recre ational use and forest fragmentation, affects the abundance of exotic plants in the Potomac River floodplain in Maryland. The author compared the frequency and diversity of exotic plants in an undisturbed forest site, a contiguous forest dis turbed by recreational use, and a fragmented forest disturbed by recreational use. She also examined the effect of flooding. The number and diversity of exotic species were greatest in disturbed, fragmented forests, less in disturbed, unfragmented forests, and lowest in intact, contiguous forest. Both forest fragmentation and recreation use appeared to facilitate inva sion by exotic plants. Even so, at least two species of exotic plants were most common in unfragmented, disturbed forest. Exotic species were more numerous away from water, possi bly because they are less well adapted to flooding than the native species. The author recommends reducing human traf fic in sensitive natural areas as a way of reducing exotic plants.

Richardson, D. M.; Williams, P. A.; Hobbs, R. J. 1994. Pine invasions in the Southern Hemisphere: determinants of spread and invadability. Journal of Biogeography. 21: 511 527.

Annotation: See section II.B.1. Page 14.

Robinson, George R.; Quinn, James F.; Stanton, Maureen L. 1995. Invasibility of experimental habitat islands in a California winter annual grassland. Ecology. 76(3): 786 794.

Annotation: The authors describe a test of the invasibility of an annual grassland community. They note that to understand species invasions through experimental testing, three kinds of information are needed: (1) historical knowledge of the eco logical community being invaded, (2) dispersal history of the invading species, and (3) knowledge of the processes that open up a community to invasion. For this study, seeds of a native poppy were introduced onto 42 previously studied plots, a subset of which consistently had higher species richness than the remaining plots. The California poppy (*Eschscholzia californica*) established and reproduced better in sites with higher species richness and less dominance of one or a few resident species, and this invader germinated better in sites with greater disturbance. The number of local species present was a more important predictor of invasibility than plot size. The authors note that results from other studies comparing species richness with the success of purposefully introduced species have been mixed, and they comment on the impor tance of chance events in determining invasibility.

Simberloff, Daniel; Von Holle, Betsy. 1999. Positive inter- actions of nonindigenous species: invasional meltdown? Biological Invasions. 1: 21 32.

Annotation: Simberloff and Von Holle discuss the state of knowledge regarding interactions among nonindigenous spe cies. They first review the concept of "environmental resistance," the process in which competitive or predatory forces oppose a newly introduced nonindigenous species. This concept of resistance has dominated studies that seek to un derstand why some introduced species survive and spread while others do not. The authors then describe a different model of invasion, which they term "invasional meltdown." This is a "…process by which a group of nonindigenous species facilitate one another's invasion in various ways, increasing the likelihood of survival and/or of ecological impact and pos sibly the magnitude of impact." The authors reviewed current literature to determine the frequency of the invasion meltdown process and to document examples. They present preliminary evidence that such a process is not uncommon, but they were unable to determine its frequency. A prevalent type of facilitative interaction appears to be that of plants modifying the habitat in such a way that other introduced species are favored over native species. The authors identified the quantification of population level impacts of nonindigenous species on one another and on native species as an urgent research need.

Stapanian, Martin A.; Sundberg, Scott D.; Baumgardner, Greg A.; Liston, Aaron. 1998. Alien plant species composition and associations with anthropogenic disturbance in North American forests. Plant Ecology. 139: 49 62.

Annotation: This paper examines the association between alien plants and human caused disturbance in seven forested regions of the United States. The authors compared alien plant diversity, cover, and origin among 279 forest plots. The diversity of alien species ranged from a low of approximately 4.5 percent in Colorado to a high of 25 percent in California across all plots. Similarly, alien cover ranged from 1.5 percent in Colorado to 25 percent in California. The majority of nonnative plants came from temperate Eurasia. The proportion of plots with at least one alien plant was significantly higher in disturbed plots only in the Northeast and Southeast. This suggests that disturbance, while facilitating the spread of exotics in some forests, is not a prerequisite for the establishment of alien species in other regions.

Stohlgren, Thomas J.; Bull, Kelly A.; Otsuki, Yuka; Villa, Cynthia A.; Lee, Michelle. 1998. Riparian zones as havens for exotic plant species in the central grasslands. Plant Ecology. 138: 113 125.

Annotation: This study adds to a growing body of literature indicating that riparian areas are highly susceptible to invasion. To determine which factors influence the distribution and abundance of native and exotic plants, the authors compared characteristics of riparian versus upland zones at various landscape scales within steppe and prairie regions of the Central United States. They found that riparian areas harbor the majority (75 to 85 percent) of both native and exotic plant species, most likely due to higher levels of light, water, and soil nitrogen near streams. Analysis at broader landscape scales (greater than 1000 m²) suggests that exotic plants tend to invade areas that have diverse plant assemblages and rich resources, such as those along streams. However, when looking at a much finer scale (less than 1 m²) within riparian areas, the authors conclude that exotics preferred areas with low native plant cover. This suggests that exotic plants use small areas that have temporary bursts of resource availability brought about by disturbance. In riparian areas, disturbance from livestock and native herbivore grazing, flooding, and erosion are common, opening temporary windows of opportunity for invasive species. Riparian areas may also be conduits of spread for exotic plants within otherwise inhospitable landscapes. Inventories of exotic plants should be a top priority for managers, and surveys should focus on riparian zones and other disturbed, nutrient rich areas. However, any control methods that are initiated within riparian zones must take into account the high native biodiversity in many infested riparian areas.

Stohlgren, Thomas J.; Binkley, Dan; Chong, Geneva W.; Kalkhan, Mohammed A.; Schell, Lisa D.; Bull, Kelly A.; Otsuki, Yuka; Newman, Gregory; Bashkin, Michael; Son, Yowhan. 1999a. Exotic plant species invade hot spots of native plant diversity. Ecological Monographs. 69(1): 25 46.

Annotation: To test the generalization that areas with diverse native floras are more resistant to invasion by exotic plants, the authors gathered and analyzed vegetation, soil and species richness data on 360 plots throughout the Rocky Mountains and Great Plains regions. Their results suggest that the opposite pattern is true; exotic plants preferentially invade areas with high native plant diversity. In areas with a high diversity of native plants, high soil fertility, and excess soil resources promote growth of nonnatives as well. Contrary to ideas previously proposed in the literature, complex and diverse plant assemblages (in other words, diversity hot spots) are not immune to exotic invasions. Further research is required to explain precisely why some areas resist invasion and others do not.

Stohlgren, Thomas J.; Schell Lisa D.; Vanden Heuvel, Brian. 1999b. How grazing and soil quality affect native and exotic plant diversity in Rocky Mountain grasslands. Ecological Applications. 9(1): 45 64.

Annotation: Several aspects of plant communities play a role in determining patterns of species richness. Consequently, the authors compared the effects of grazing, soil characteristics, and climate at multiple spatial scales in grazed and ungrazed sites. At the landscape scale (1,000 m² plots), there were not significant differences in native species richness or the numbers of native and exotic species between grazed and ungrazed sites. The authors develop five broad generalizations concerning current levels of grazing in Rocky Mountain grasslands: (1) grazing appears to have little effect on native species richness at the landscape scale (greater than 1,000 m); (2) grazing probably does not contribute to the accelerated spread of most nonnative plants at landscape scales; (3) grazing does affect local plant species, life form composition and cover, but considerable spatial variation exists; (4) soil characteristics, climate, and disturbances appear to have a greater effect on plant species diversity than do current grazing levels; and (5) few plant species show consistent, directional responses to either grazing or the termination of grazing. Although grazing did not appear to facilitate the spread of exotics on a landscape scale in this study, the authors caution that grazing may nonetheless lead to the replacement of native species by exotic species at the local scale. Biomes that evolved under different grazing pressures also may respond differently to grazing than do Rocky Mountain grasslands.

Weaver, T.; Woods, B. 1986. Exotic plant invasions of _Thuja-Tsuga_ habitats, N. W. Montana. In: Thomas, Jr., L. K., ed. Proceedings: conference on science in the National Parks, 1986, Vol. 5: Management of exotic species in natural communities; 1986 July 13 18; Fort Collins, CO. U.S. National Park Service and The George Wright Society: 111 119.

Annotation: The authors surveyed invasive plants in three areas within _Thuja/Oplopanax_ and _Tsuga/Clintonia_ habitat types on the west side of Glacier National Park: (1) climax forests, (2) roadside areas of minimal disturbance undergoing secondary succession, and (3) areas along highly disturbed road cuts undergoing primary succession. Climax forests contained no invasive plants, whereas invasive plants increased from areas with secondary succession to those with primary succession. Invasive plants increased with the level of disturbance. Disturbed roadside areas appear to act as corridors for exotic plant invasions.

3. Mediated Dispersal

Benninger-Truax, Mary; Vankat, John L.; Schaefer, Robert L. 1992. Trail corridors as habitat and conduits for movement of plant species in Rocky Mountain National Park, Colorado, USA. Landscape Ecology. 6(4): 269 278.

Annotation: This study sought to determine whether trail corridors provide habitat for certain plant species and act as conduits for the movement of species. The authors found that the distance from trail edges, the degree of trail use, and the distance from trailheads significantly affected the species composition of plants. Species either colonized or were inhibited from trail corridors, depending on their growth habits and tolerance of disturbance. The species richness of exotics was greatest closest to trails. Based on these findings, it appears that trails (particularly those that experience heavy use) facilitate the spread of nonnative plants into wilderness and other natural areas.

Crawley, Michael J. 1987. What makes a community invasible? In: Gray, A. J.; Crawley, M. J.; Edwards, P. J., eds. Colonization, succession and stability. Oxford, England: Blackwell Scientific Publications: 429 453.

Annotation: See section II.B.2. Page 16.

Deering, Ryan H.; Vankat, John L. 1998. Forest colonization and developmental growth of the invasive shrub *Lonicera maackii*. American Midland Naturalist. 141: 43 50.

Annotation: Animal related dispersal can be extremely important in plant invasions. The authors document patterns of demography and growth in a local population of the invasive shrub, Amur honeysuckle (*Lonicera maackii*), within an isolated woodlot in Ohio. The invader was probably introduced several different times by birds dispersing seeds into the woodlot. A 10 year lag phase between its arrival on the plot and its subsequent population explosion resulted from both a delay in seed production before initial colonizers reached maturity and an additional bird mediated seed dispersal into the area as other nearby source populations of honeysuckle expanded.

Greenberg, Cathryn H.; Crownover, Stanley H.; Gordon, Doria R. 1997. Roadside soils: a corridor for invasion of xeric scrub by nonindigenous plants. Natural Areas Journal. 17(2): 99 109.

Annotation: See section II.B.2. Page 17.

Heywood, Vernon H. 1989. Patterns, extents and modes of invasions by terrestrial plants. In: Drake, J. A.; Mooney, H. A.; di Castri, F.; Groves, R. H.; Kruger, F. J.; Rejmánek, M.; Williamson, M., eds. Biological invasions: a global perspective. Chichester, England: John Wiley and Sons: 31 60.

Annotation: See section II.A. Page 10.

Johansson, Mats E.; Nilsson, Christer; Nilsson, Elisabet. 1996. Do rivers function as corridors for plant dispersal? Journal of Vegetation Science. 7: 593 598.

Annotation: This study evaluated the importance of dispersal for determining plant species frequencies and distributions along rivers. The authors compared long distance floating and short distance floating seed species with their frequencies along the riverbanks of 10 rivers in northern Sweden. Four reference sites in the same region were also chosen for comparison with areas where other mechanisms act as dispersal agents. Water dispersal capacities of different species were determined by buoyancy records, which are more reliable than morphological characteristics because buoyant seeds float longer distances. This study found a positive relationship between floating capacity and frequency of species along riverbanks. It also showed that seeds of vegetatively dispersed species, rather than wind or animal dispersed species, had higher floating capacities than other seeds. The results of this study indicate that water dispersal has a role in structuring the riparian flora, and species distribution patterns can be explained based on seed dispersal characteristics. The authors conclude that a large number of interactive factors determine the variation in species frequency along riverbanks and that dispersal properties should be considered because species with effective means of water dispersal are generally more frequent along river corridors. The authors indicate that rivers seem to function as corridors for plant dispersal and suggest that continuous river corridors are important for maintaining regional biodiversity.

Lacey, John R.; Wallander, Rosie; Olson-Rutz, Kathrin. 1992. Recovery, germinability, and viability of leafy spurge (*Euphorbia esula*) seeds ingested by sheep and goats. Weed Technology. 6(3): 599 602.

Annotation: See section III.E.5. Page 51.

Lonsdale, W. M.; Lane, A. M. 1994. Tourist vehicles as vectors of weed seeds in Kakadu National Park, Northern Australia. Biological Conservation. 69: 277 283.

Annotation: The number of introduced vascular plant species in parks and reserves is positively correlated with human visitation rate. This study investigates a possible cause of this correlation, the transport of seeds on tourist vehicles. During one year, samples of the number of seeds and the number occurrences of seeds were taken from tourist vehicles entering Kakadu National Park to determine whether or not these vehicles acted as vectors of weed seeds into the Park. The results indicated that nearly half the vehicles carried no seeds, and the majority of those carrying any seeds at all had less than three. However, the nine Kakadu weed species found on cars were found on three times as many sites throughout Kakadu as other weeds, implying that cars may be partly responsible for weed infestation in the Park. Despite the latter finding, the authors feel that resources would be wasted on the prevention of seeds entering the Park through tourist vehicles because of the low density of seeds they found on tourist vehicles, the high probability that seeds entering the Park on a car will also leave it in the same way, and the generality that most germinating seeds do not survive to maturity. They conclude that the concentration on early detection and eradication of any established weed stands within the Park would be a more effective use of resources.

Mack, Richard N.; Lonsdale, W. Mark. 2001. Humans as global plant dispersers: getting more than we bargained for. BioScience. 51(2): 95 102.

Annotation: This review describes some of the motivations that lead to the introduction of plants both transoceanically and throughout a new range. The authors briefly describe the role of natural plant dispersers (wind, ocean currents, and so forth), concluding that as transoceanic vectors, these forces play an insignificant role relative to human mediated dispersal. However, they can facilitate spread once nonindigenous species are established. A three phase historical perspective on weed dispersal is presented (accidental, utilitarian, and aesthetic). We are presently in this aesthetic phase where the international market for ornamental, nonindigenous plants is problematic and many introductions are deliberate. The authors also describe how the epidemiology of weed spread is similar to that of other biological invaders, particularly parasites, and they describe the biological factors that promote invasions on land (for example, seed dispersal by birds, storms, and floods). Natural areas are not immune to dispersing invasives (visitors' vehicles and clothing play a role), but the importance of this vector has not been adequately studied. It is the initial weed establishment by humans within a potential new range that most concerns these authors.

Marcus, W. Andrew; Milner, Gary; Maxwell, Bruce. 1998. Spotted knapweed distribution in stock camps and trails of the Selway-Bitterroot Wilderness. Great Basin Naturalist. 58(2): 156 166.

Annotation: Packstock feed and droppings may be important vectors of invasive plants. The authors' survey of the Bitterroot portion of the Selway Bitterroot Wilderness in Montana revealed spotted knapweed (*Centaurea maculosa*) on five of five trails and in six of 30 stock camps surveyed. Over 95 percent of knapweed found along trails was within 0.5 km of trailheads. Spotted knapweed only occurred below 1700 m, within 7.5 km of the trailhead, and within 4.6 m of trails. It was associated with stock camps that had an open canopy, increased disturbance to soils and vegetation, and increased campsite development (although this was confounded with elevation). Within campsites, there was no difference in knapweed abundance between areas used by stock and those used by humans. The authors suggest that field surveys are essential for assessing the actual extent and severity of infestations in wilderness and for deciding on appropriate control measures. Weed removal by backcountry rangers, volunteers, or visitors may be effective for controlling knapweed in the Selway Bitterroot Wilderness.

Novak, Stephen J.; Mack, Richard N. 2001. Tracing plant introduction and spread: genetic evidence from *Bromus tectorum* (cheatgrass). BioScience. 51(2): 114 122.

Annotation: The authors reconstruct the introduction and spread of cheatgrass into North American and other regions by the use of multiple lines of independent evidence (historical records, herbarium specimens, and molecular genetic techniques). These combined techniques offer a more complete understanding of both the source populations and the invasion process. Determining the native range of an invasive plant facilitates identification of natural constraints to persistence, including the potential response to biological controls. The historical evidence suggests that in the West, cheatgrass was introduced from Europe almost simultaneously at several disparate sites, and range expansion was rapid. Despite reductions in genetic variation that occurred following the initial introduction of new populations, the authors found higher levels of genetic variation in naturalized populations than in native populations. This is likely a result of multiple introductions in the same location. The authors conclude that there were broadly similar circumstances leading to the worldwide introduction of this species, and these introductions were closely tied to European movements. This article chronicles a portion of their findings in this extensive and ongoing effort.

Pearson, Dean E.; Ortega, Yvette K. 2001. Evidence of an indirect dispersal pathway for spotted knapweed, *Centaurea maculosa*, seeds, via deer mice, *Peromyscus maniculatus*, and great horned owls, *Bubo virginianus*. Canadian Field Naturalist. 115(2): 354.

Annotation: Seeds of invasive species can be distributed indirectly by moving through the food chain. Pearson and Ortega suggest that predators may act as indirect dispersal agents of spotted knapweed (*Centaurea maculosa*) when they prey on some deer mice. Interestingly, the relevant deer mice accidentally ingest the seeds while preying on gall fly larvae, the biological control of spotted knapweed.

Sallabanks, Rex. 1993. Fruiting plant attractiveness to avian seed dispersers: native vs. invasive *Crataegus* in western Oregon. Madroño. 40(2): 108 106.

Annotation: This study tested whether dispersal by fruit eating birds is responsible for the invasive spread of a nonnative hawthorn (*Crataegus monogyna*). The author compared the attractiveness of fruits from native and nonnative hawthorns to American robins (*Turdus migratorius*), the primary dispersal agent. The fruits of the nonnative hawthorn were more attractive to robins than those of the native hawthorn and were more likely to be dispersed farther.

Schiffman, Paula M. 1997. Animal-mediated dispersal and disturbance: driving forces behind alien plant naturalization. In: Luken, James O.; Thieret, John W., eds. Assessment and management of plant invasions. New York, NY: Springer Verlag: 87 94.

Annotation: This paper focuses on the importance of animal mediated dispersal and disturbance in nonnative plant invasions. The author discusses ways in which animals contribute to both reproduction and dispersal in exotic plants. Although changes in natural disturbance regimes are almost invariably related to human activities, animals may also change the level or intensity of disturbance and thereby facilitate invasions. The author first provides examples of how indigenous and nonindigenous animals have altered disturbance regimes and facilitated plant invasions. Schiffman then discusses the complex interactions that can develop between native animals and nonnative plants. According to the author, managers of natural areas should identify and evaluate all possible exotic plant seed dispersers and attempt to minimize human impacts that lead to greater dispersal by animals. Descriptive, comparative, and experimental studies of relationships between animals and exotic plants will be valuable for enabling managers to control established exotics.

Tyser, Robin W.; Worley, Christopher A. 1992. Alien flora in grasslands adjacent to road and trail corridors in Glacier National Park, Montana (USA). Conservation Biology. 6(2): 253 262.

Annotation: This paper depicts the invasion of native grasslands adjacent to roads and backcountry trails by exotic plants. The number of exotic plant species declined as the distance from roads increased, suggesting that these exotics are suc cessfully invading from roadside areas. Results regarding trail sides were less clear. Species richness of nonnative plants did not decrease with increasing distance from trails. The unex pectedly high levels of exotic species 100 m from trails sug gest that these exotics may have been introduced in off trail areas. The results of this study suggest that even native grasslands with low levels of grazing and human distur bance are vulnerable to invasion by exotic plants. The au thors make numerous management recommendations regarding road construction, the intentional introduction of alien species, roadside vegetation management programs, proactive control polices, and livestock related activities in nature reserves.

Vellend, Mark. 2002. A pest and an invader: white-tailed deer (*Odocoileus virginianus* Zimm.) as a seed dispersal agent for honeysuckle shrubs (*Lonicera* L.). Natural Areas Journal. 22: 230 234.

Annotation: When trying to accurately predict invasion dy namics, it is necessary to give significance to all possible dis persal modes. In Eastern North America, the white tailed deer (*Odocoileus virginianus*) is a principal seed disperser. East ern North America is increasingly inhabited by alien invasive honeysuckle shrubs (*Lonicera* spp.). Honeysuckle invasion has negative effects on native plants and has high potential for inhibiting forest regeneration and decreasing native plant di versity. White tailed deer increase this potential as an effec tive and important dispersal agent for bush honeysuckles. The collection of 72 white tailed deer pellet groups from five ma ture mixed hardwood stands provided data that indicate that white tailed deer are a disperser of viable honeysuckle seeds. Historically, birds have been reported as the principal dispersal agent for seeds of invasive honeysuckle, and this paper exam ines the relative importance of white tailed deer, versus birds, as dispersal agents. The author also uses data from the lit erature and makes his comparisons by examining the feed ing, digestive, and movement behaviors of deer and birds. He concludes that white tailed deer are also a principal dis perser of honeysuckle seeds, and because of their high den sities and daily movements of up to a kilometer or more, white tailed deer have considerable potential for contrib uting to the spread of invasive honeysuckles as well as other plant species.

C. Effects of Invasive Plants

Understanding the ecological impacts of invasive species is important for assessing the level of threat they pose to a particular ecosystem. Some invasive plants directly alter the distribution, abundance or composition of native species by outcompeting or hybridizing with natives. Others affect na tive plants indirectly by altering the composition of native herbivores. Some invasive plants alter the frequency, inten sity, or scale of ecosystem level processes with which native species have evolved. These include disturbances such as fire (D'Antonio and Vitousek 1992), as well as changes in hydrol ogy (Gordon 1998), soil properties (Vitousek 1986, 1992), and nutrient cycling (Cameron and Spencer 1989). Vitousek (1986, 1992) reviews the effects of invasive plants on ecosystem prop erties, and Walker and Smith (1997) provide an overview of

community level impacts of invasive plants. Mack and D'Antonio (1998) review how invasive plants alter fire re gimes. The papers in the first section below discuss the direct and indirect impacts of invasive species on ecosystem struc ture and function, and the threat that these impacts pose to communities of native plant species.

Invasive plants affect not only the plant communities they invade, but also the wildlife associated with those communi ties. The second section addresses the effects of invasive plants on wildlife. Most publications have documented lower densi ties of native wildlife species in invaded areas (Disney and Stokes 1976, Slobodchikoff and Doyen 1977, Reynolds 1979, Mazzotti and others 1981, Bock and others 1986, Johnson and others 1994, and Trammell and Butler 1995). However, some studies show that certain native species tolerate (Whelan and Dilger 1992) or even preferentially use altered habitats (Macdonald and Frame 1988 and Johnson and others 1994). These studies address birds, ungulates, rodents, lizards, and arthropods.

1. Effects on Plant Communities and Ecosystem Processes

Abbott, Richard J. 1992. Plant invasions, interspecific hy bridization and the evolution of new plant taxa. Trends in Ecology and Evolution. 7(12): 401 405.

Annotation: Hybridization in plants can lead to the forma tion of new species in several ways. The author presents and reviews evidence for plant species of recent hybrid origin and concludes that widespread introductions of exotic plants have contributed to this phenomenon. Of greatest interest to con servation and management is the evidence presented that hy brids of native and introduced species may acquire locally adapted genes or gene complexes that allow them to rapidly colonize and establish within the habitat of the native parent.

Aplet, G. H. 1990. Alteration of earthworm community biomass by the alien *Myrica faya* in Hawai'i. Oecologia. 82: 414 416.

Annotation: This paper presents an example of how an inva sive species can alter ecosystem level processes (in this case, nutrient cycling) and facilitate invasions by other nonnative species. The author examined changes in earthworm popula tions resulting from the invasion of *Myrica faya*, a nitrogen fixing exotic plant, in Hawai'i. The biomass of exotic earthworms was significantly higher in stands of *Myrica* than in open submontane forests or native rainforest stands. Earth worm biomass was also significantly higher under individual *Myrica* trees than under native trees. Interactions between the nitrogen additions by *Myrica* and the litter processing by earth worms are likely to exacerbate ecosystem changes in areas where *Myrica* is invading.

Brooks, Matthew L.; Pyke, David A. 2001. Invasive plants and fire in the deserts of North America. In: Galley, Krista E. M.; Wilson, Tyrone P., eds. Proceedings of the invasive species workshop: the role of fire in the control and spread of invasive species. Fire Conference 2000: The First National Congress on Fire Ecology, Prevention, and Management. Misc. Pub. No. 11, Tall Timbers Research Station, Tallahassee, FL: 1 14.

Annotation: The relationship between invasive species and fire in desert communities is complex. Invasive species such as cheatgrass (*Bromus tectorum*) may increase fire intensity and frequency by filling interspaces in the plant community, which allows fires to spread more easily across landscapes. Competition for limited resources may be especially impor tant in desert ecosystems, and invasive plants may be better competitors for soil water than some natives. Indeed the pres ence of red brome (*Bromus madritensis* ssp. *rubens*), Medi terranean grass (*Schismus* spp.), and red stemmed filaree (*Erodium cicutarium*) can reduce the biomass of native seed lings. Moreover, increasing fire frequencies may aid invasion and promote long term effects in desert ecosystems. Histori cally, fires occurred in the Great Basin at 30 to100 year in tervals and were extremely rare in deserts. These intervals have shortened recently to as few as 5 years in parts of the Great Basin. Short fire intervals are also emerging in the Mojave and Sonoran Deserts. Although perennial grasses and annuals may survive fires, woody shrubs and cacti are often killed by fire, especially recurrent fires. As a result, recurring fires are causing high diversity native desert shrublands to be converted to low diversity nonnative grasslands with homogenous nu trient distributions and water cycles. On the other hand, na tive perennial grasslands are being converted to shrublands by fire suppression and livestock grazing, and changing rela tively homogenous nutrient environments into environments where nutrient resources are heterogeneously distributed. These habitat type conversions may indirectly impact wild life species associated with these deserts. Land managers should be cautious with the use of fire as a tool to control invasive species. Although fire may be effective at reducing some species, such as cheatgrass, effects may be only partial or temporary. In addition, fire may promote establishment of other invasive species. Fire resistant plants may act to slow or stop wildfires, but they must be highly competitive to main tain their function of disrupting fuel continuity (especially in cheatgrass dominated sites). Revegetation after wildfires may be difficult in desert systems because of limited seed avail ability. Restoration efforts may improve the odds that desir able plants become established by using a diversity of native species sown at high densities, and reducing soil nitrogen lev els with sucrose treatments immediately after fire.

Cameron, Guy N.; Spencer, Stephen R. 1989. Rapid leaf decay and nutrient release in a Chinese tallow forest. Oecologia. 80: 222 228.

Annotation: Litterfall from introduced trees can alter soil composition and may increase the productivity of local eco systems by adding limiting nutrients. The authors studied the effects of litter decomposition on nutrient availability in areas of introduced Chinese tallow trees (*Sapium sebiferum*) that have invaded coastal prairies along the Texas Gulf Coast. Tal low tree leaves decayed more rapidly than those of native de ciduous trees and contributed elements that often limit soil productivity.

D'Antonio, Carla M.; Vitousek, Peter M. 1992. Biological invasions by exotic grasses, the grass/fire cycle, and global change. Annual Review of Ecology and Systematics. 23: 63 87.

Annotation: This paper focuses on the potentially devastat ing global consequences of exotic grass invasions. In the in troduction, the authors list three ways that biological invasions can affect ecosystems: by altering (1) the system level rates of resource supply, (2) trophic structure, or (3) disturbance regimes in the invaded area. After describing global geographic patterns of alien grass invasions, they outline the potential ef fects on ecosystems that occur via competition for light, nu trients, and water. Such changes can lead to the slowing or altering of plant succession and may increase the proportion of the Earth's surface that remains in an early successional stage. In addition, grasses can also alter geomorphological processes and microclimate. Finally, the authors discuss the interactions between grass invasions and fire (which they view as the most significant effect of alien grasses on ecosystems) and some potential global consequences of this interaction.

Gordon, Doria R. 1998. Effects of invasive, nonindigenous plant species on ecosystem processes: lessons from Florida. Ecological Applications. 8(4): 975 989.

Annotation: Invasive plants may out compete natives not only due to superior competitive ability but also by altering the properties of the ecosystem they invade in their favor. To test this idea, the author reviewed data on the impacts of 31 inva sive plant species on ecosystem processes in Florida. Between 40 and 65 percent of these species greatly affected soil struc ture, hydrology, biogeochemistry, and/or disturbance regimes. Specific impacts of each species are reviewed in detail. Eco system restoration therefore, will require not only controlling invasive plants, but also reestablishing natives and the eco system processes under which they evolved.

Grace, James B.; Smith, Melinda D.; Grace, Susan L.; Collins, Scott L.; Stohlgren, Thomas J. 2001. Interactions between fire and invasive plants in temperate grasslands of North America. In: Galley, Krista E. M.; Wilson, Tyrone P., eds. Proceedings of the invasive species workshop: the role of fire in the control and spread of invasive species. Fire Con ference 2000: The First National Congress on Fire Ecology, Prevention, and Management. Misc. Pub. No. 11, Tall Tim bers Research Station, Tallahassee, FL: 40 65.

Annotation: See section II.B.2. Page 17.

Huenneke, Laura F. 1996. Ecological impacts of invasive plants in natural resource areas. Proceedings: Western So ciety of Weed Science; 1996 March 11 14; Albuquerque, NM. Newark, CA: 49: 119 121.

Annotation: This paper describes a number of ecological ef fects brought on by nonnative plant invasions, including the direct displacement of native plants, negative effects on wild life, increased soil erosion, changes in soil chemistry and nu trient cycles, changes in hydrology and stream flow, and changes in disturbance regimes. The author emphasizes that the absence of disturbance is no guarantee against invasion, and that the early detection and control of invasive species is an important part of an invasive plant management strategy.

Hughes, Flint; Vitousek, Peter M.; Tunison, Timothy. 1991. Alien grass invasion and fire in the seasonal submontane zone of Hawai'i. Ecology. 72(2): 743 746.

Annotation: See section II.B.2. Page 18.

Keeley, Jon E. 2001. Fire and invasive species in Mediter ranean-climate ecosystems of California. In: Galley, Krista E. M.; Wilson, Tyrone P., eds. Proceedings of the invasive species workshop: the role of fire in the control and spread of invasive species. Fire Conference 2000: The First National

Congress on Fire Ecology, Prevention, and Management. Misc. Pub. No. 11, Tall Timbers Research Station, Tallahassee, FL: 81 94.

Annotation: See section II.B.2. Page 18.

Lambrinos, John G. 2000. The impact of the invasive alien grass *Cortaderia jubata* (Lemoine) Stapf on an endangered Mediterranean-type shrubland in California. Diversity and Distributions. 6(5): 217 231.

Annotation: Since its introduction as an ornamental in the late 19th century, the perennial tussock grass *Cortaderia jubata* has invaded plots of maritime chaparral from central Califor nia to southern Oregon. Lambrinos studies the effect *C. jubata* has had on the diversity and composition of plant and animal communities. He finds that while *C. jubata* invasion has not decreased vegetation diversity overall, it has decreased the diversity of native species and replaced shrubland with less structurally complex grassland. This decrease in structural complexity has in large part been responsible for a decrease in arthropod and rodent density and diversity. The author explores the implications of this conversion of chaparral to grassland and examines the factors contributing to the *C. jubata* inva sion. He also discusses the need for research quantifying the effects invasive plants have on ecosystem structure and diversity.

Ley, Ruth E.; D'Antonio, Carla M. 1998. Exotic grass in vasion alters potential rates of N fixation in Hawaiian woodlands. Oecologia. 113: 179 187.

Annotation: Invasion of native dry tropical forests by exotic grasses in Hawai'i has resulted in an unnatural regime of fre quent and severe fires, and in turn, the large scale conversion of native forests to exotic grasslands. Such grasslands are then maintained by the continuing fire cycle. The authors found that this change in vegetation from native forest to grassland substantially decreased nitrogen fixation and therefore the level of nitrogen in the soil. They concluded that invasive species have greatly altered nutrient cycling in these forests and that large reductions in soil nitrogen will lead to impoverishment of the native ecosystem.

Macdonald, I. A. W.; Frame, G. W. 1988. The invasion of introduced species into nature reserves in tropical savan nas and dry woodlands. Biological Conservation. 44: 67 93.

Annotation: See section I. Page 7.

Macdonald, Ian A. W.; Loope, Lloyd L.; Usher, Michael B.; Hamann O. 1989. Wildlife conservation and the inva sion of nature reserves by introduced species: a global per spective. In: Drake, J.A.; Mooney, H.A.; di Castri, F.; Groves, R. H.; Kruger, F. J.; Rejmánek, M.; Williamson, M., eds. Bio logical invasions: a global perspective. Chichester, England: John Wiley and Sons: 215 255.

Annotation: This review article covers a broad range of top ics related to the effects of invasive, introduced species (plants, animals, and fungal species) on ecosystem structure and func tion within nature reserves around the world. It chronicles the known extent of invasion to reserves, although this has been measured for only a handful of introduced species. The au thors note that in one study the annual number of visitors to a reserve was the only characteristic that affected the number of introduced vascular plants. Examples of the effects of

introductions on various types of ecosystem functions, includ ing alteration of geomorphological processes, biogeochemi cal cycling, hydrological cycles, and fire regimes, are provided. The authors also provide examples of invasions that have pre vented native species recruitment. Finally, examples are in cluded from a variety of nature reserves in which introduced plants and animals are implicated in faunal extinction, a much more common occurrence on islands than continents. The au thors stress the need for managers to: (1) eliminate changes in disturbance regimes to which the native biota have not evolved, (2) establish management priorities, (3) initiate monitoring so that invasions can be detected in their early stages, (4) imple ment followup actions to prevent reestablishment, and (5) con duct cost benefit analyses of control techniques.

Mack, Michelle C.; D'Antonio, Carla M. 1998. Impacts of biological invasions on disturbance regimes. Trends in Ecol ogy and Evolution. 13(5): 195 198.

Annotation: The evidence clearly indicates that individual invasive species have altered ecosystems by changing distur bance regimes. Indeed, invasive species have changed distur bance regimes in both disrupted and intact systems. The authors focus on three common mechanisms by which this happens. Many invaders change the amount of physical disturbance, by enhancing or suppressing fire, or by increasing or decreasing soil disturbance. Other invaders (primarily animals) have them selves become disturbance agents. Finally, certain invading species act either to intensify or ameliorate the effects of dis turbance on the system. Most of the studies reviewed demon strated that altering disturbance regimes promotes invasive species and contributes to the demise of at least a portion of the native biota. In their conclusion, the authors caution that the continued movement of species around the globe by hu mans will only compound the negative effects of disturbance and invasions on ecosystems.

McArthur, E. Durant; Romney, Evan M.; Smith, Stanley D.; Tueller, Paul T., comps. 1990. Proceedings: symposium on cheatgrass invasion, shrub die-off and other aspects of shrub biology and management; 1989 April 5–7; Las Ve gas, NV. Gen. Tech. Rep. INT 276. Ogden, UT: U.S. Depart ment of Agriculture, Forest Service, Intermountain Research Station. 351 p.

Annotation: The invasion of cheatgrass (*Bromus tectorum*) over large areas of the Intermountain West is implicated in recent large scale die offs of ecologically important native shrubs such as big sagebrush. The first and second sections of this report describe ongoing problems with the invasion of cheatgrass into rangelands of the Western United States as well as different strategies to counteract the problem.

Mooney, H. A.; Cleland, E. E. 2001. The evolutionary im pact of invasive species. Proceedings of the National Acad emy of Science. 98(10): 5446 5451.

Annotation: The structure and function of most of the Earth's systems have been altered by human activities. Even protected areas are affected by global changes in the abiotic environ ment (for example, atmosphere and climate) and biotic com munities. Although fluctuations in biota are natural processes, the *rate* of exchange of species among the Earth's regions has increased dramatically, especially within the last 50 years. These invasive species can alter basic evolutionary processes. Mooney and Cleland review the impacts both invasive plants and animals may have on native species. Evolutionary trajec tories may be altered if any the following situations occur: native species adapt to or hybridize with invasives, invasive species cause behavioral or trait shifts in natives, native spe cies are ecologically displaced or excluded by invasives, mu tualistic relationships between native species are disrupted by invasives, or invasive species cause the extinction of native species.

Olson, Bret E. 1999a. Impacts of noxious weeds on eco logic and economic systems. In: Sheley, Roger L.; Petroff, Janet K., eds. Biology and management of noxious rangeland weeds. Corvallis, OR: Oregon State University Press: 4 18.

Annotation: See section II.A. Page 11.

Peters, Erin F.; Bunting, Stephen C. 1994. Fire conditions pre- and postoccurrence of annual grasses on the Snake River plain. In: Monsen, Stephen B.; Kitchen, Stanley G., eds. Proceedings: ecology and management of annual range lands; 1992 May 18 20; Boise, ID. Gen. Tech. Rep. INT GTR 313. Ogden, UT: U.S. Department of Agriculture, Forest Service, Intermountain Research Station: 31 36.

Annotation: The majority of this paper consists of a review of historical documents describing the vegetation and fre quency of fires on the lower Snake River Plain prior to the introduction of exotic annual grasses. The authors first briefly describe the history of cheatgrass (*Bromus tectorum*) and medusahead (*Taeniatherum caput medusae*) introductions. Then they detail the effects of these exotic grasses on fire re gimes and biological communities in Snake River Plain sage brush grasslands. The introduction of these exotic annual grasses has disrupted historical disturbance regimes and suc cessional patterns. With each successive fire, annual grasses have become more dominant, and the fire free interval has decreased. The continued conversion of sagebrush rangeland to annual grasslands due to fires has homogenized the land scape, decreased species diversity, and increased the severity and extent of fires.

Randall, John M. 1996. Weed control for the preservation of biological diversity. Weed Technology. 10(2): 370 383.

Annotation: The author lists numerous examples of habitat dominance and the displacement of native plants by exotic species. Examples include invasive nonnative trees, shrubs, vines, and herbaceous species. See full annotation in section I. Page 7.

Richburg, Julie A.; Dibble, Alison C.; Patterson, III, Will iam A. 2001. Woody invasive species and their role in al tering fire regimes of the Northeast and Mid-Atlantic States. In: Galley, Krista E. M.; Wilson, Tyrone P., eds. Pro ceedings of the invasive species workshop: the role of fire in the control and spread of invasive species. Fire Conference 2000: The First National Congress on Fire Ecology, Preven tion, and Management. Misc. Pub. No. 11, Tall Timbers Re search Station, Tallahassee, FL: 104 111.

Annotation: This paper reviews the ecology of some of the most common woody invasive species in the Northeast and discusses the physiological basis for management. Many of these species' seeds are dispersed by birds (for example, Japa nese barberry [*Berberis thunbergii*] and Russian olive [*Elaeagnus angustifolia*]) and so have the potential to invade a variety of habitats from long distances. The authors summarize

their review in a table including the geographic regions where each invasive species is a problem, how the species is dis persed, the effects the species has on the native community, and methods to control the species. The effects of manage ment actions may vary depending on season and the carbohy drate reserves of the targeted plant. Carbohydrate reserves are depleted during bud break, replenished during the growing season, and used gradually in respiration during the dormant season. Therefore, as a result of woody plant physiology, fire during the dormant season may be ineffective at controlling these invasive species and may actually increase production. Fires timed to defoliate plants during reserve replenishment may reduce growth and impact the plant's vigor during the following growing season.

Schmitz, D. C.; Schardt, J. D.; Leslie, A. J.; Dray, Jr., F. A.; Osborne, J. A.; Nelson, B. V. 1993. The ecological im pact and management history of three invasive alien aquatic plant species in Florida. In: McKnight, Bill N., ed. Biological pollution: the control and impact of invasive ex otic species. Indianapolis, IN: Indiana Academy of Science: 173 194.

Annotation: Invasive aquatic plants have severely affected freshwater habitats around the world. In this paper, the au thors thoroughly review the history, biology, and manage ment of water hyacinth (*Eichhornia crassipes*), water lettuce (*Pistia stratiotes*), and hydrilla (*Hydrilla verticillata*) in vasions in Florida. These three species arrived in the late 1800s and by the mid 1950s, had expanded throughout the State. These invasions led to blockage of inland waterways, local extinctions of native aquatic plants, increased sedi mentation, deoxygenation of benthic zones, bioaccumula tion of heavy metals, and in some cases widespread fish kills. Even so, these species may provide increased cover from predators for juvenile game fish. The impacts of these aquatic invasives on the physical structure, chemistry, and hydrology of freshwater habitats is well documented, but their biological effects remain poorly understood. Control efforts now focus on long term maintenance control rather than eradication.

Simberloff, Daniel; Von Holle, Betsy. 1999. Positive inter actions of nonindigenous species: invasional meltdown? Biological Invasions. 1: 21 32.

Annotation: See section II.B.2. Page 20.

Slobodchikoff, C. N.; Doyen, John T. 1977. Effects of *Ammophila arenaria* on sand dune arthropod communi ties. Ecology. 58: 1171 1175.

Annotation: See section II.C.2. Page 31.

Steenkamp, H. E.; Chown, S. L. 1996. Influence of dense stands of an exotic tree, *Prosopis glandulosa* Benson, on a savanna dung beetle (Coleoptera: scarabaeinae) assem blage in southern Africa. Biological Conservation. 78(3): 305 311.

Annotation: See section II.C.2. Page 31.

Vitousek, Peter M. 1986. Biological invasions and ecosys tem properties: can species make a difference? In: Mooney, Harold A.; Drake, James A., eds. Ecology of biological inva sions of North America and Hawaii. New York, NY: Springer Verlag: 163 176.

Annotation: A single introduced species could have dramatic effects on ecosystem structure and function, but what kinds of species are these and why are their effects so large? The significant effects of introduced species that add a new structural life form, such as floating aquatic weeds or *Tamarix* (in other words, salt cedar, tamarisk) in the desert Southwest, are well documented. Other introduced species that have the potential to alter large scale structure and processes are those that change soil properties (for example, nitrogen fixing shrubs), disturbance regimes (for example, fire prone annual grasses), primary productivity, or the intensity of herbivory, and those that have periods of growth different from natives, either seasonally or during the process of succession. Effects on ecosystems are most pronounced when invaders cause changes that reinforce the original divergence from preinvasion conditions.

Vitousek, Peter M. 1992. Effects of alien plants on native ecosystems. In: Stone, Charles P.; Smith, Clifford W.; Tunison, J. Timothy, eds. Alien plant invasions in native ecosystems of Hawai'i: management and research. Honolulu, HI: Cooperative National Park Resources Studies Unit. University of Hawaii Press: 29 41.

Annotation: This easy to follow overview paper describes how invasive plants can change ecosystem level properties such as the large scale functioning of ecosystems, community structure, and population dynamics. Through a number of examples, Vitousek offers evidence that the characteristics of individual invading species are important at the ecosystem level. He concentrates on cases where plants invade undisturbed native ecosystems or where they alter the successional course when invading disturbed areas. He specifically describes how different life forms can change ecosystems processes, how plants can alter resource acquisition and use (for example, nitrogen fixation), and how invasive plants can interact with disturbance vectors (fire and animals).

Vitousek, Peter M.; Walker, Lawrence R.; Whiteaker, Louis D.; Mueller-Dombois, Deter; Matson, Pamela A. 1987. Biological invasion by *Myrica faya* alters ecosystem development in Hawaii. Science. 238: 802 804.

Annotation: This article highlights how individual species, in this case a nitrogen fixing tree, can alter ecosystem dynamics. *Myrica faya* invaded young volcanic substrates in Hawaii that previously contained no native plants with nitrogen fixing symbiosis, and it significantly increased both the amount of nitrogen entering these sites and the overall biological availability of nitrogen. This in turn altered the character of the native forest ecosystem. The authors note that similar effects of biological invasions on ecosystem level properties are likely more common on oceanic islands where the native flora are relatively depauperate, and successful invasions are common place. Exotic species that alter ecosystem level properties may not only compete with or consume native plants, but may alter the underlying nature of the invaded area.

Walker, Lawrence R.; Smith, Stanley D. 1997. Impacts of invasive plants on community and ecosystem properties. In: Luken, James O.; Thieret, John W., eds. Assessment and management of plant invasions. New York, NY: Springer Verlag: 69 86.

Annotation: The authors outline a community level approach for assessing and managing impacts of nonnative plant invasions. Because invasive plants alter both community level properties (in other words, primary productivity, species diversity, vegetation structure) and processes (in other words, disturbance regimes, succession patterns, nutrient cycles, hydrology), they argue that restoring native ecosystems involves understanding how such properties and processes have been altered by invasion. Five main topics are discussed: primary productivity, soil nutrients, ground water and salinity, disturbance regimes, and community dynamics. For each, the authors provide a conceptual background, recommend ways to measure change in the attribute due to invasion, and discuss management concerns. Case studies of the fayatree in Hawai'i and tamarisk in the Southwestern United States are used to illustrate changes in, and ways of restoring, the attributes that comprised biological communities prior to invasion.

Whisenant, Steven G. 1990. Changing fire frequencies on Idaho's Snake River Plains: ecological and management implications. In McArthur, E. Durant; Romney, Evan M.; Smith, Stanley D.; Tueller, Paul T., comps. Proceedings symposium on cheatgrass invasion, shrub die off, and other aspects of shrub biology and management; 1989 April 5 7; Las Vegas, NV. Gen. Tech. Rep. INT 276. Ogden, UT: U.S. Department of Agriculture, Forest Service, Intermountain Research Station: 4 10.

Annotation: Before the arrival of Euro American settlers, large contiguous fires burned in the sagebrush steppe at 30 to 70 year intervals. Small areas within this ecosystem, however, burned at higher frequencies: about every 15 to 40 years. Whisenant presents evidence that the conversion of sagebrush steppe to a system dominated by cheatgrass (*Bromus tectorum*) is not only a result of increased fire frequency but also an increase in the continuity of fine fuel. Cheatgrass relative abundance is directly related to the amount of fine fuel and the fire frequency in the system. More important, this fine fuel reduces the interspacing between plants resulting in fires that can burn more frequently and over larger areas than in the evolutionary history of native perennials. For example, sagebrush can reestablish from seed after fire but requires at least 4 to 6 years before the new plants can produce seeds. Short fire returns quickly remove these types of plants from the system permitting the expansion of cheatgrass and other annuals and increasing fire frequency. As these fine fuels expand, the high species diversity of the sagebrush steppe (that historically resulted from small, infrequent fires) disappears. Whisenant suggests management strategies include the greenstrip program (planting fire resistant plants to slow or stop fires) developed by the Bureau of Land Management to reduce the size of fires and overall to reduce the frequency of fires.

Woods, Kerry D. 1997. Community response to plant invasion. In: Luken, James O.; Thieret, John W., eds. Assessment and management of plant invasions. New York, NY: Springer Verlag: 56 68.

Annotation: The author reviews the effects of invasive species on relatively undisturbed communities in order to identify (1) characteristics of invasive species that lead to predictable levels and types of community change, (2) characteristics of communities that make them susceptible to invasion, and (3) differences in the community level impacts of invasions with and without human induced disturbance. After critically reviewing potential mechanisms and case studies, including those found in the paleoecological record, the author concludes that the effects of disturbance and invasion often cannot be separated. The kinds of invasive species most likely to dramatically change community structure or func tion are those that outcompete native species for light during critical life history stages, those with alternative morpho lo gies and life history strategies, and those that utilize resources in a novel way. However, such invaders remain difficult, if not impossible, to identify before an invasion has occurred. Similarly, this research failed to identify any previously unre ported characteristics of communities that distinguish them as being more prone to invasion than others. For now, care fully documenting the impacts of current invasions is probably the most effective way to successfully predict com munity level effects of future invasions.

2. Effects on Wildlife

Anderson, Bertin. W.; Higgins, Alton; Ohmart, Robert D. 1977. Avian use of saltcedar communities along the lower Colorado River Valley. In: Johnson, R. R.; Jones, D. A., eds. Importance, preservation and management of riparian habi tat: a symposium; 1977 July 9; Tucson, AZ. Gen. Tech. Rep. RM 43. Fort Collins, CO: U.S. Department of Agriculture, Forest Service, Rocky Mountain Forest and Range Experi ment Station: 128 136.

Annotation: This study suggests that saltcedar (*Tamarix chinensis*) communities support a lower diversity of birds than do native communities in certain seasons. Tall dense saltcedar stands were preferred over younger saltcedar stands and were used by nesting doves and several other bird species typically associated with native cottonwood willow communities.

Bock, Carl E.; Bock, Jane H.; Jepson, Karen L.; Ortega, Joseph C. 1986. Ecological effects of planting African lovegrasses in Arizona. National Geographic Research. 2(4): 456 463.

Annotation: This paper documents the effect of exotic grasses on the native flora and fauna of Southwestern United States rangelands. The authors compare the flora and fauna of native grasslands dominated by exotic lovegrasses (Lehmann lovegrass [*Eragrostis lehmanniana*] and Boer lovegrass [*E. curvula*]). Native grasslands supported a signifi cantly greater variety and abundance of indigenous grasses, herbs, shrubs, grasshoppers, rodents, and birds. Twenty spe cies of plants and animals were more abundant in the native grasslands, whereas only three indigenous animal species were more abundant in the exotic grasslands. Based on their re sults, the authors conclude that the practice of planting exotic lovegrasses to revegetate damaged rangelands is a less desir able land management alternative than giving native grass lands the time and opportunity they need to recover from past land uses.

Brandt, C. A.; Rickard, W. H. 1994. Alien taxa in the North American shrub-steppe four decades after cessation of live-stock grazing and cultivation of agriculture. Biological Conservation. 68(2): 95 106.

Annotation: See section II.B.2. Page 15.

Disney, H. J. de S.; Stokes, A. 1976. Birds in pine and na-tive forests. Emu. 76: 133 138.

Annotation: In this study, stands of introduced Monterey pine (*Pinus radiata*) in Australia supported dramatically fewer breeding bird species and a lower total abundance of birds than did native wet sclerophyll forest. This provides an ex ample where the presence of a nonnative plant species nega tively affected the abundance of native bird species. However, native *dry* sclerophyll forest had greater diversity and abun dance of birds than pine stands. The authors emphasize that the presence of nest cavities in older, large size class trees in native forest contributed to the differences in the numbers and abundance of breeding species.

Ellis, Lisa M. 1995. Bird use of saltcedar and cottonwood vegetation in the Middle Rio Grande Valley of New Mexico, U.S.A. Journal of Arid Environments. 30: 339 349.

Annotation: This study compared avian use of native cotton wood (*Populus fremontii*) and exotic saltcedar (*Tamarix chinensis*) riparian habitats in spring, summer, and fall. Bird species richness was similar in both habitats, but species com position varied. More species were unique to cottonwood sites than to saltcedar sites in all seasons. Results may have been confounded by the occurrence of a saltcedar subcanopy in the cottonwood sites and the occurrence of a patch of mature cot tonwoods in one of the two saltcedar sites. Certain birds in the saltcedar site that contained cottonwoods showed a preference for the native vegetation, suggesting that the presence of scat tered native plants may enhance the value of saltcedar stands for some birds. Continued conversion of native cottonwood habitat to saltcedar could result in declines of certain species of birds.

Ellis, Lisa M.; Crawford, Clifford S.; Molles, Jr., Manuel C. 1997. Rodent communities in native and exotic ripar-ian vegetation in the Middle Rio Grande Valley of central New Mexico. Southwestern Naturalist. 42(1): 13 19.

Annotation: This study examined the effect of exotic ripar ian vegetation on rodent communities by comparing species composition and richness in stands of native cottonwoods (*Populus fremontii*) and exotic saltcedar (*Tamarix chinensis*). Species richness was greater in saltcedar, which contained several species typically associated with dry upland or grass land habitats. This finding may reflect the greater proximity of the two saltcedar stands to upland source habitats. Addi tional confounding factors may have been the presence of a saltcedar subcanopy in the cottonwood sites, different trap ping designs and effort in the two types of stands, and experi mental flooding in one of the cottonwood stands during one of the study years.

Hunter, William C.; Ohmart, Robert D.; Anderson, Bertin W. 1988. Use of exotic saltcedar (*Tamarix chinensis*) by birds in arid riparian systems. Condor. 90(1): 113 123.

Annotation: This paper compares avian use of saltcedar in three different regions. All bird groups (categorized by food preferences and time of occurrence in area) showed high use of saltcedar in all seasons in one study area but minimal use in the other two areas. In one of the latter two areas, densities of several summer visiting insectivores have shown marked de clines since the proliferation of saltcedar. Differences in use of saltcedar by birds may be related to the native vegetation that was present prior to invasion by saltcedar, to vegetation currently co occurring with saltcedar, and/or to climatic gra dients between the study areas.

Johnson, K. H.; Olson, R. A.; Whitson, T. D.; Swearingen, R. J.; Kurz, G. L. 1994. Ecological implications of Russian knapweed infestations: small mammal and habitat associations. In: Proceedings: 47th annual meeting of the Western Society of Weed Science; 1994 March 14 17; Coeur d'Alene, ID. Newark, CA: 47: 98 101.

Annotation: This study compared small mammal communi ties in sites infested with Russian knapweed (*Centaurea repens*) and in uninfested sites. Numbers of native kangaroo rats and ground squirrels were lower in infested sites than in uninfested sites (but one of the selected "uninfested" sites was dominated by other types of weeds). Species associated with disturbed, early successional, or weed infested areas, such as deer mice and western harvest mice, were more abundant on knapweed sites.

Lambrinos, John G. 2000. The impact of the invasive alien grass *Cortaderia jubata* (Lemoine) Stapf on an endangered Mediterranean-type shrubland in California. Diversity and Distributions. 6(5): 217 231.

Annotation: The decrease in structural complexity caused by a *Cortaderia jubata* invasion has in large part been respon sible for a decrease in arthropod and rodent density and diver sity. See full annotation in section II.C.1. Page 26.

Macdonald, I. A. W.; Frame, G. W. 1988. The invasion of introduced species into nature reserves in tropical savan nas and dry woodlands. Biological Conservation. 44: 67 93.

Annotation: This paper discusses the invasibility and current invasion status of savanna reserves and presents several case studies. In one preserve in South Africa, the prolific fruiting of invasive plants attracted so many native frugivores that such plants may indirectly be interfering with the dispersal of na tive fruiting plants. See full annotation in section I. Page 7.

Macdonald, Ian A. W.; Loope, Lloyd L.; Usher, Michael B.; Hamann O. 1989. Wildlife conservation and the inva sion of nature reserves by introduced species: a global per spective. In: Drake, J. A.; Mooney, H. A.; di Castri, F.; Groves, R. H.; Kruger, F. J.; Rejmánek, M.; Williamson, M., eds. Bio logical invasions: a global perspective. Chichester, England: John Wiley and Sons: 215 255.

Annotation: Examples are included from a variety of nature reserves in which introduced plants and animals are impli cated in faunal extinction. See full annotation in section II.C.1. Page 26.

Mazzotti, Frank J.; Ostrenko, Witold; Smith, Andrew T. 1981. Effects of the exotic plants *Melaleuca quinquenervia* and *Casuarina equisetifolia* on small mammal populations in the eastern Florida Everglades. Florida Scientist. 44(2): 65 71.

Annotation: This paper compares numbers of three sympat ric rodents in exotic and native habitats in the Everglades. The authors found that exotic Australian pine (*Casuarina equisetifolia*) habitats had depauperate rodent communities. In contrast, each of the rodent species was common in habi tats consisting wholly or partly of another exotic, the paperbark tree (*Melaleuca quinquenervia*). Based on these findings, the authors point out that not all exotic habitats are equal in their ability to sustain native wildlife and therefore must be evalu ated separately when assessing their suitability for animal

populations. Despite the presence of rodents in the *Melaleuca* habitat, the authors also stress that this type of habitat may not be "good" for wildlife because numbers of rodents were lower in *Melaleuca* than they have been found to be in native com munities.

Pearson, Dean E.; Ortega, Yvette K; McKelvey, Kevin S.; Ruggiero, Leonard F. 2001. Small mammal community composition, relative abundance, and habitat selection in native bunchgrass of the Northern Rocky Mountains: im plications for exotic plant invasions. Northwest Science. 75(2): 107 117.

Annotation: Small mammals play important species specific roles in ecosystem function and may influence invasions by nonnative plants (for example, create disturbed sites, consume nonnative plants and seeds, disperse seeds, and depredate bio logical control agents). Because little is known of small mam mal ecology in bunchgrass habitat, potential impacts to these animals from invasive establishment are difficult to predict. Results from a one season, live trapping survey at three pris tine valley bunchgrass sites provide baseline data on small mammal composition (deer mice, montane voles, and mon tane shrews; consistent among sites), relative abundance (deer mice highest, followed by voles), and habitat use (varied among species and between sexes). Invasive species may differen tially affect these mammals; the habitat generalist deer mice may be favored over the habitat and dietary specialist voles and shrews following weed invasions.

Reynolds, Timothy D. 1979. Response of reptile popula tions to different land management practices on the Idaho National Engineering Laboratory Site. Great Basin Natu ralist. 39(3): 255 262.

Annotation: This study compared reptile populations in grazed and ungrazed habitats dominated either by native sagebrush (*Artemisia tridentata*) or by exotic crested wheatgrass (*Agro pyron cirstatum*). The relative density of two lizard species was significantly greater in each of the sagebrush sites than in either of the crested wheatgrass sites. The results suggest that the continued conversion of sagebrush dominated habitats to crested wheatgrass will have a negative impact on popula tions of native lizards.

Rice, Peter M.; Toney, J. Christopher; Bedunah, Donald J.; Carlson, Clinton E. 1997a. Elk winter forage enhance ment by herbicide control of spotted knapweed. Wildlife Society Bulletin. 25(3): 627 633.

Annotation: This paper compares estimates of elk winter for age on knapweed (*Centaurea maculosa*) infested plots that were treated with herbicides versus untreated plots. Three years after spraying, herbicide treated plots had 47 percent more elk winter forage than did the untreated plots. The authors suggest that, because the amount of elk winter range is declin ing as a result of development in the Northern Rockies, con trol of knapweed may become increasingly important because remaining areas will need to be optimally productive.

Schmidt, Kenneth A.; Whelan, Christopher J. 1999. Ef fects of exotic *Lonicera* and *Rhamnus* on songbird nest predation. Conservation Biology. 13(6): 1502 1506.

Annotation: American robins (*Turdus migratorius*) and wood thrushes (*Hylocichla mustelina*) both nest in native and nonnative shrubs. Robin nests built in the exotic species experienced higher depredation than those built in comparable native shrubs or trees. This may be due to the lower nest height, absence of sharp thorns, and open branch architecture of the exotic species. Despite higher depredation, robins increased their use of *Lonicera maackii* during the study, perhaps be cause it leafs out earlier. Wood thrush nests in *Lonicera* expe rienced higher depredation than nests in a pooled group of native species, but rates were similar to nests in a native spe cies of comparable height and stature. Nonnative plants may serve as ecological traps; if birds nest in nonnative shrubs in high densities, this could decrease the overall nesting success of the population. If depredation rates are indeed higher in nonnative plants, restoring native shrub species may benefit local avian communities.

Slobodchikoff, C. N.; Doyen, John T. 1977. Effects of *Ammophila arenaria* on sand dune arthropod communi- ties. Ecology. 58(5): 1171 1175.

Annotation: Invasions by beach grass (*Ammophila arenaria*) planted to stabilize coastal sand dunes altered both the species diversity and community structure of native, sand dwelling arthropods. Even relatively low amounts of exotic beach grass cover severely depressed the species diversity and abundance of arthropods. The tendency of introduced beach grass to form monocultures, which dis place native vegetation and result in drastic reductions in native arthropods, make introducing beach grass to stabi lize dunes in parks inappropriate.

Steenkamp, H. E.; Chown, S. L. 1996. Influence of dense stands of an exotic tree, *Prosopis glandulosa* Benson, on a savanna dung beetle (Coleoptera: scarabaeinae) assem- blage in southern Africa. Biological Conservation. 78(3): 305 311.

Annotation: This paper examines the effect of an invasive exotic mesquite on dung beetle assemblages in Southern Af rica. Species richness of dung beetles was greater in undis turbed savanna than in areas with exotic mesquite trees. The savanna habitat also exhibited a more equitable species distri bution. Furthermore, beetle biomass, numbers, species domi nance, diversity, and size distributions differed between the two habitats. Larger dung beetles showed an aversion to non native habitat. Similarly, rare species declined or were absent from the mesquite thickets. Changes in dung beetle commu nities brought about by the invasion of exotic species could lead to changes in nutrient cycling and deteriorations of range land quality.

Stromayer, Karl A. K.; Warren, Robert J.; Johnson, A. Sydney; Hale, Philip E.; Rogers, Carolyn L.; Tucker, Chris- topher L. 1998. Chinese privet and the feeding ecology of white-tailed deer: the role of an exotic plant. Journal of Wildlife Management. 62(4): 1321 1329.

Annotation: The authors examined the seasonal importance of exotic Chinese privet (*Ligustrum sinense*) browse and fruit in the food habits of white tailed deer. Privet was an important component of the fall and winter diets of deer and may serve as a nutritional buffer during years of acorn scarcity. Although privet may increase the winter carrying capacity of deer, the authors caution that its tendency to form dense monospecific stands may reduce regional biodiversity and negatively affect deer during the spring and summer.

Thompson, Michael J. 1996. Winter foraging response of elk to spotted knapweed removal. Northwest Science. 70(1): 10 19.

Annotation: This study compared the foraging activity, diet, and distribution of elk on a portion of winter range treated to control spotted knapweed (*Centaurea maculosa*) versus on untreated portions still infested with knapweed. Although elk walked indiscriminately through adjacent treated and untreated stands, they foraged almost exclusively in the treated stands. In addition, a higher proportion of elk used the treated stand after spotted knapweed was controlled. The author suggests that elk managers consider preexisting range conditions, knap weed densities, the occurrence of current and desired elk dis tributions, and the probability of adequate rainfall for grass growth after herbicide application when planning knapweed removal on elk winter range.

Trammell, Michael A.; Butler, Jack L. 1995. Effects of ex- otic plants on native ungulate use of habitat. Journal of Wildlife Management. 59(4): 808 816.

Annotation: This study used pellet group densities to esti mate habitat use by bison, elk, and deer within four infested and four noninfested grassland habitats. The authors also used twig counts and measurements to estimate use of browse in woodlands with and without infestations of leafy spurge (*Eu phorbia esula*). Native ungulates browsed in leafy spurge in fested habitats significantly less than in noninfested habitats. This reduction in use may be due to lower production of for age in these sites, to avoidance of leafy spurge areas, or both. The author cautions that the invasion of exotic plants may reduce the overall carrying capacity of an area, which in turn may lead to overbrowsing and overgrazing of uninfested sites. Such a disturbance could facilitate the invasion of uninfested lands from surrounding infested sites, thereby accelerating the invasion process.

Whelan, Christopher J.; Dilger, Michael L. 1992. Invasive, exotic shrubs: a paradox for natural area managers? Natu ral Areas Journal. 12(2): 109 110.

Annotation: See section III.F. Page 54.

Willard, E. Earl; Bedunah, Donald J.; Marcum, C. Les. 1988. Use and preference of spotted knapweed by elk and mule deer on two winter ranges in western Montana. In: Impacts and potential impacts of spotted knapweed (*Centau rea maculosa*) on forest and range lands in western Montana. Missoula, MT: Forest and Conservation Experiment Station, University of Montana; Final Report: 128 186.

Annotation: This study assessed the forage value of spotted knapweed by examining both its chemical composition and its amount of use by wintering elk and deer. Chemical analy sis showed that knapweed remains nutritious throughout win ter. Knapweed appeared to be consumed by elk and deer predominantly because of its high availability. Nevertheless, its use was low overall and limited to the protein rich flower tops. Because of their greater dependence on grasses, elk are likely to be more negatively affected by the proliferation of knapweed than mule deer.

Williams, Peter A.; Karl, Brian J. 1997. Unravelling the relationship between weeds and birds. Forest Bird. 283: 42 47; February.

Annotation: This study assesses the relative importance of fruit bearing introduced weeds and native plants to small birds in three forest patches in New Zealand. Exotic plants increased the availability of fruit during winter. Nevertheless, 99 per cent of the fruit eaten by two native frugivores still came from native plants. In contrast, introduced blackbirds and thrushes ate similar proportions of native and exotic fruits. The introduced species spent most of their time in urban areas, where many of the exotic plant species originate, and moved among a wider range of vegetation types than did native birds. As a result, introduced birds were more likely to dis perse the seeds and promote the spread of nonnative plants than were native birds.

Wilson, Scott D.; Belcher, Joyce W. 1989. Plant and bird communities of native prairie and introduced Eurasian vegetation in Manitoba, Canada. Conservation Biology. 3(1): 39 44.

Annotation: Nonnative Eurasian plants not only replaced the native plant community in a North American mixed grass prai rie, but also changed the composition of the native bird com munity. The plant species composition differed significantly between patches of native prairie and patches dominated by exotic species. In addition, the species richness of the native prairie was twice that of the exotic patches. While all but one bird species were found in both vegetation types, two species were significantly more abundant in the native vegetation.

Overall, the species composition of the bird community dif fered significantly between native and exotic patches. Such differences were probably related to the effects of exotic plants on the food supply and structure of the nesting habitat.

Wright, Anthony L.; Kelsey, Rick G. 1997. Effects of spot ted knapweed on a cervid winter-spring range in Idaho. Journal of Range Management. 50(5): 487 496.

Annotation: Contrary to other studies, the authors found no evidence of a dramatic reduction in the carrying capacity of wilderness winter spring range used by elk, mule deer, and white tailed deer after infestation with spotted knapweed (*Cen taurea maculosa*). Densities of cervids in infested areas were greater than or equal to densities in areas comprising native bunchgrasses and sedges. White tailed deer made little use of the native sites. Knapweed seedheads and rosette leaves were eaten by all three cervid species, and the energy and protein content of rosettes was similar to that of preferred native food plants. The authors acknowledge that other ecosystem factors may obscure the effects of knapweed on cervid populations. They conclude with examples of situations they believe jus tify or do not justify extensive campaigns to control knap weed on cervid winter spring ranges. In addition, they comment on the importance of preventing and controlling new invasions, establishing biocontrol agents, preventing invasions of successively detrimental species, and educating wilderness users and management personnel.

III. Invasive Plant Management

A. Management Planning

Management of invasive plants in nature reserves, including designated wilderness areas, has become a major concern. Overviews describing how to develop comprehensive management plans can be found in Hobbs and Humphries (1995), Schwartz and Randall (1995), and Hiebert (1997). Specifically, Hiebert (1997) discusses the steps comprising the decisionmaking process, and Schwartz and Randall (1995) include a flow chart describing management actions and the decisions confronting land managers. Sheley and Petroff (1999) also present a thorough approach to weed management that will be applicable to some wilderness areas. Information specifically related to planning control strategies can be found in section III.E.1., Developing and Prioritizing Control Strategies. Additionally, for examples of Federal management planning efforts, see section IV.A., Sample Environmental Impact Statements.

Anderson, Bruce; Wotring, Ken. 2001. Invasive plant management along wild rivers: are we stewards, guardians, or gardeners? International Journal of Wilderness. 7: 25 29.

Annotation: See section III.E.1. Page 41.

Hiebert, Ronald D. 1997. Prioritizing invasive plants and planning for management. In: Luken, James O.; Thieret, John W., eds. Assessment and management of plant invasions. New York, NY: Springer Verlag: 195 212.

Annotation: Hiebert outlines the necessary steps and tools needed to manage invasive nonnative plants in natural areas. Because funds are typically limited and technology for controlling exotic plants remains inadequate, the author stresses the importance of concentrating management efforts on those species posing the greatest threat to rare and endemic plants and to landscape level ecological processes. After emphasizing the importance of using an analytical approach to prioritize management efforts, Hiebert outlines and discusses the steps in the decisionmaking process and discusses a variety of decisionmaking tools. In doing so, he walks managers through the necessary steps involved in initiating an exotic plant control program. Finally, he presents a ranking system, used by the National Park Service, to help prioritize which exotics

should be controlled. Shaped by ecological principles and management constraints, the system ranks exotic species based on their present level of impact and their innate potential to become serious pests. In addition, the system separately rates the feasibility of control of each exotic species to allow managers to weigh the threat or impact of each plant versus the cost and feasibility of controlling it. The scheme also incorporates the level of urgency for controlling each plant. Hiebert provides the ranking system and its numerical ratings in a usable outline format and also provides a detailed description of and justification for the various components in the system.

Hobbs, Richard J.; Humphries, Stella E. 1995. An integrated approach to the ecology and management of plant invasions. Conservation Biology. 9(4): 761 770.

Annotation: The authors suggest that the current focus in the field of invasive plant management on the characteristics and control of invading species is inadequate. They recommend a more integrated approach that includes prevention, detection, early control, and ecosystem, rather than single species management. Identifying and dealing with the factors that cause ecosystems to become more invasible will lead to more successful control efforts than will current attempts to control each species that has already become a major problem. The authors provide a framework for setting management priorities based on the relative degree of site disturbance and on each site's relative production or conservation value. Finally, they suggest that changes in human activities related to plant introductions and use, in land use, and in timing of control measures are required before plant invasions can be adequately addressed.

Madsen, John D. 1997. Methods for management of nonindigenous aquatic plants. In: Luken, James O.; Thieret, John W., eds. Assessment and management of plant invasions. New York, NY: Springer Verlag: 145 171.

Annotation: This paper focuses on the steps involved in developing and implementing a nonindigenous aquatic plant management program. The author discusses six components of a successful, integrated management plan: prevention, assessment, site specific management, evaluation, monitoring, and education. In addition, he describes the five major management techniques currently being used to control exotic aquatic plants: biological, chemical, mechanical, physical, and institutional.

National Invasive Species Council. 2001. Meeting the invasive species challenge: national invasive species management plan. 80 p. (*Note: This document is available online at http://www.invasivespecies.gov/council/nmp.shtml.*)

Annotation: As directed by Executive Order 13112, the National Invasive Species Council developed this national management plan for invasive species. The plan provides a blueprint from which the U.S. Federal agencies, along with their partners, can work to minimize the significant impacts of invasive species. It includes general sections on leadership and coordination, prevention, early detection and rapid response, control and management, restoration, international cooperation, research, information management, and education and public awareness. The Federal agencies are currently working to integrate this plan's recommendations into their invasive species management programs.

Ricciardi, Anthony; Steiner, William W. M.; Mack, Richard N.; Simberloff, Daniel. 2000. Toward a global information system for invasive species. BioScience. 50: 239 244.

Annotation: After illustrating the threats of the growing frequency and impacts of biological invasions worldwide, the authors assert that both early detection and effective control of invasive species depend upon the availability of up to date information that keeps pace with new invasion threats. The authors note that retrieving critical information about the spread, impact, and control of invasive species has always been a difficult problem because much of this information is not widely accessible, is of variable quality, and has diffuse distribution. These factors ultimately limit the ability of managers to combat invasions. This problem is further compounded when managers' information needs increase beyond a regional or national scale. The authors respond to this problem by proposing the development of an Internet based global information system that would provide comprehensive and readily accessible information to aid with the monitoring, risk assessment, and control of invasive species. A workshop was convened to discuss the creation of an Internet global information system for invasive plant species. The goals of this workshop were to address management and research needs regarding invasive plants, and to identify the information system's key elements. This paper briefly outlines and summarizes the ideas that resulted from the conference. It also emphasizes how an Internet based information system would benefit managers who need comprehensive, up to date, and readily available information to effectively allocate limited resources toward the prevention and eradication of invasive species. This paper points out that an Internet global information system has the potential to play a large role in enhancing public awareness of invasion problems, which is critical because virtually all of species introductions are caused by human activity.

Schwaller, Ann E. 2001. Social dimensions of exotic weed management in National Forests and adjacent communities. Missoula, MT: The University of Montana. Thesis. 179 p.

Annotation: Exotic weed invasions have been viewed routinely as a biological problem, yet for effective weed management it is also necessary to understand the social aspects of this problem. Historically, the problem of weed invasion has been viewed through a utilitarian lens because many agricultural and range interests are affected by weeds. This project addresses the modes of traditional resource management and the agency/community relationship. It emphasizes that because the establishment and spread of exotic weeds in Western National Forests is currently a dominant issue for land managers, the challenge is to understand the human beliefs and values surrounding exotic weeds. Social dimensions influence the public and land managers' interpretations and communications about the issue of exotic weeds with regard to forest management. The author of this project, by conducting in depth interviews, develops an approach for assessing these dimensions. A variety of themes were uncovered in the interviews, but the emphasis of the study deals mainly with themes concerning weed issues and public relationships with land management agencies. These themes included weed awareness, public participation, cooperation, the role of information and how it is used and communicated, and understanding differences in worldviews. This paper provides insight into the social dimensions of exotic weed management and identifies the disengagement between land managers and the public. A better understanding by managers of the human attitudes and changing social conditions will increase their ability to anticipate social needs, implement weed awareness within the public, and break down the barriers to communication and to cooperative efforts on weed management issues.

Schwartz, Mark W. 1997. Defining indigenous species: an introduction. In: Luken, James O.; Thieret, John W., eds. Assessment and Management of Plant Invasions. New York, NY: Springer Verlag: 7 17.

Annotation: Often the first step in developing a management plan is determining whether a particular plant species is indigenous, yet the criteria used have been lacking. After presenting various definitions of native species, Schwartz illustrates the complexities involved in trying to pinpoint specific time horizons and locations on which to base classifications of indigenous species. He then discusses the ways in which mechanisms for changes in species distributions, including direct and indirect human intervention, have complicated our ability to distinguish what is native from what is exotic. Finally, he emphasizes the importance of developing explicit conservation goals to facilitate the classification of indigenous versus nonindigenous species when approaching management problems.

Schwartz, Mark W.; Randall, John M. 1995. Valuing natural areas and controlling nonindigenous plants. Natural Areas Journal. 15(2): 98 100.

Annotation: This brief paper consists primarily of a response to an article by J. O. Luken (Natural Areas Journal 14: 295 299), which argues that biological invasions are viewed negatively because of current social values and that additional scientific study is needed before adopting eradication programs. Countering Luken, the authors underscore the importance of preventing exotic plant introductions and eradicating newly established infestations. They then provide an outline of a strategy for nonnative plant management and include a flow chart describing management actions and decisions confronting natural land managers.

Sheley, Roger L.; Petroff, Janet K. 1999. Biology and management of noxious rangeland weeds. Corvallis, OR: Oregon State University Press: 438 p.

Annotation: Although the focus of this book is on Western rangelands, it contains a great deal of information useful and relevant to natural area managers. The book is divided into two sections. The first 11 chapters deal with the theory, concepts, and principles of rangeland weed management and are organized in the same way that one might develop a weed management plan. These chapters include information on the impacts of weeds, surveying, mapping, and monitoring weeds, coordinating weed management planning, evaluating costs and benefits, integrated management techniques, preventing invasions, and detecting and controlling small infestations. In addition, section I includes chapters on three management techniques grazing, biological control, and chemical control and one chapter on revegetation. The second section consists of 25 chapters describing 29 of the most serious noxious weed species in Western United States rangelands. Each of these chapters includes sections with information on invasive plant identification, origin and distribution, invasive potential, ecological and economic impacts, biology and ecology, and management options.

B. Preventing Invasions

Once nonnative plants are widespread, they are often extremely difficult, if not impossible, to eradicate. For this reason, preventing invasions is an important step in invasive plant management. Prevention can occur at several levels. Preventing the importation of known invasive plants at State and National levels will require new legislation that improves regulation and funding for inspections at ports of entry (Van Driesche and Van Driesche 2001). At the local level, educating wilderness users about the ecological and economic impacts of invasive plants and taking measures to prevent new invasions will be valuable (Kummerow 1992, Sheley and others 1999b, Asher and others 2001). Van Driesche and Van Driesche (2001) provide a review of historical and current approaches to preventing invasive species introductions in the United States and outline new ideas for more effective prevention. Reichard and White (2001) review preventing horticultural introductions, and Campbell (2001) assesses prevention through international trade regulations.

Asher, Jerry E.; Dewey, Steve; Johnson, Curt; Olivarez, Jim. 2001. Reducing the spread of invasive exotic plants following fire in Western forests, deserts, and grasslands. Abstract. In: Galley, Krista E. M.; Wilson, Tyrone P., eds. Proceedings of the invasive species workshop: the role of fire in the control and spread of invasive species. Fire Conference 2000: The First National Congress on Fire Ecology, Prevention, and Management. Misc. Pub. No. 11, Tall Timbers Research Station, Tallahassee, FL: 102 103.

Annotation: This extended abstract discusses the potential for invasive species to become established following wild land fire. Diffuse knapweed (*Centaurea diffusa*), squarrose knapweed (*C. virgata*), and rush skeletonweed (*Chondrilla juncea*), for example, can exploit postfire conditions by setting seed within 6 weeks of fire. The authors suggest 10 considerations for both prescribed and wildfire management including: (1) ensuring that the National Environmental Policy Act (NEPA) process is adequate, (2) establishing procedures

that prevent weed transport, (3) delineating infestations, and (4) involving cooperators. After fires, (5) consider postfire herbicide treatment, (6) build the cost of weed control into fire rehabilitation plans, (7) ensure weeds get priority, (8) use only weed free mulch, (9) conduct repeated followup surveys, and (10) develop and implement a weed control strategy. When planning prescribed burns, the authors suggest first surveying the entire area for weed populations including checking with local weed experts and adjacent landowners. Also, enlist the advice of agency weed coordinators. Time the burns to reduce seed production of existing weeds. Make sure all equipment and personnel are weed free. Finally, make sure that the appropriate NEPA process and requirements for weed control are addressed.

Campbell, Faith Thompson. 2001. The science of risk assessment for phytosanitary regulation and the impact of changing trade regulations. BioScience. 51(2):148 153.

Annotation: This article examines current U.S. policies governing the structure and implementation of invasive species prevention programs from an international trade perspective. Following a brief discussion of the role of international trade in importing new invasives, the author describes a science based phytosanitary program to replace what many consider inadequate U.S. safeguards. Because knowledge of invasives is limited and biological invasions are generally irreversible, Campbell advocates two goals: "if in doubt, keep it out" and "guilty until proven innocent." She highlights the challenges and frustrations in developing protective laws while working under the constraints of international trade agreements; such agreements restrict the right of the United States to protect itself from repeated introductions from damaging plants. She mentions flaws in both specific agreements to which the country is party and also certain policies and procedures of the USDA Animal and Plant Health Inspection Service. Relying too heavily on the slow and data hungry process of risk assessment is particularly troubling. Campbell urges scientists to press for changes to current pest/weed exclusion strategies.

Daehler, Curtis C.; Strong, Donald R. 1996. Status, prediction and prevention of introduced cordgrass *Spartina* spp. invasions in Pacific estuaries, USA. Biological Conservation. 78: 51 58.

Annotation: The Pacific coast has a limited number of marine estuaries that are critical areas of habitat for native wild life, particularly migratory shorebirds. Various species of cordgrass, *Spartina* spp., have invaded some of these estuaries and dramatically changed their structure, hydrology, and ecology. The authors identified sites vulnerable to invasion and predicted the spatial spread of cordgrass within each site. To prevent additional invasions, they recommend preventing illegal cordgrass introductions and promoting vigilant monitoring and eradication efforts. These marine estuaries have several parallels with many wilderness areas: habitats are still relatively pristine and support unique native species communities, they are crucial for maintaining key wildlife species at a continental scale, and due to intensifying human use, are increasingly subject to invasions.

Kummerow, Max. 1992. Weeds in wilderness: a threat to biodiversity. Western Wildlands. 18: 12 17; Summer.
Annotation: See section I. Page 6.

Reichard, Sarah H. 1997. Prevention of invasive plant introductions on national and local levels. In: Luken, James O.; Thieret John W., eds. Assessment and management of plant invasions. New York, NY: Springer Verlag: 215 227.

Annotation: This chapter reviews both current legislation enacted to prevent exotic plant invasions and methods for pre dicting which plants are likely to invade natural areas. See full annotation in section III.C. Page 38.

Reichard, Sarah Hayden; White, Peter. 2001. Horticulture as a pathway of invasive plant introductions in the United States. BioScience. 51(2): 103 113.

Annotation: In this extensive review, the authors describe the influence of the horticultural industry as an introducer of in vasive plants. They note that the majority of woody invasive plants in the United States were introduced via horticulture, and they suggest introduction methods have changed little in 400 years. Plant expeditions, botanical gardens, nurseries, and international and garden club seed exchanges are all pathways to invasive introductions. The authors review the U.S. legal restrictions on plant introductions, noting that such restric tions are few. The United States has no regulations requiring screening for invasive capability prior to introduction. There fore, the authors argue for an updated and more streamlined statutory framework that would allow for effective exclusion, detection, and management. Methods to minimize the dan gers of inappropriate plant introductions (including risk as sessment) are thoroughly described. This paper includes results from a survey of nursery customers, concluding that consum ers strongly prefer not to purchase invasives, need more in formation, and wish to be informed regarding invasiveness before purchasing. Finally, the authors discuss how ecology, conservation, and horticulture can work together, and they refute in detail common objectives made by horticulturists. They note that land managers should encourage public par ticipation in weed control in natural areas to increase famil iarity with invasives.

Schmitz, Don C.; Simberloff, Daniel . 2001. Biological in vasions: a growing threat. Issues in Science and Technol ogy. 13: 33 40.

Annotation: This review article chronicles the severe prob lems associated with invasive plants and animals and the in adequate steps presently being taken to address such problems. The authors describe the ecological costs that accompany these invasions, providing examples of how invasive species have dramatically altered ecosystem character and processes. They also document the challenges to preventing new invasions, highlighting the ineffective laws, regulations, and competing political interests within and among State and Federal agen cies. Current review processes clearly fail to screen potential detrimental species. The authors describe more effective strat egies, including the use of "whitelists" (permitting importa tion only if the species poses a low risk) to replace the current "blacklists" (permitting importation until the species is de clared undesirable). They emphasize the need to coordinate control efforts (through government and nongovernment en tities), provide adequate funding, and consider entire ecosys tems in this endeavor. They mention Florida as an example of a State that has made progress coordinating and funding pre vention and control strategies. Schmitz and Simberloff call for the Federal government to provide leadership, coordinating

management activities on public lands, and help educate the public, and they suggest that an analog to the Center for Disease Control could be initiated for invasive plants and animals.

Sheley, Roger; Manoukian, Mark; Marks, Gerald. 1999a. Preventing noxious weed invasion. In: Sheley, Roger L.; Petroff, Janet K., eds. Biology and management of noxious rangeland weeds. Corvallis, OR: Oregon State University Press: 69 72.

Annotation: This short chapter outlines and discusses strate gies for preventing the spread of noxious weeds. An effective prevention program typically depends on a combination of methods that limit weed spread. The authors discuss preven tion measures such as limiting weed seed dispersal, contain ing neighboring weed infestations, minimizing soil disturbances, detecting and eradicating weed introductions early, establishing competitive grasses, and properly manag ing competitive grasses.

Van Driesche, Jason; Van Driesche, Roy. 2001. Guilty un til proven innocent: preventing nonnative species invasions. Conservation Biology in Practice. 2(1): 8 17.

Annotation: Preventing, rather than responding to, invasions by nonnative species has become a central focus for conser vation. This article reviews the importance of prevention, low and high risk importation patterns, and the limited ability of inspections to detect, and therefore prevent, accidental intro ductions. They discuss two conceptual approaches to preven tion, "dirty lists" and "clean lists." After reviewing U.S. policy on nonnative species, they conclude that the current "dirty list" approach is inferior, both from an economic and ecological standpoint, to a carefully planned "clean list" approach. They outline different immediate regulatory actions that could greatly reduce the number of harmful species introductions, as well as a recent executive order that has begun that process.

C. Predicting Invasive Potential, Spread, and Distribution

Management units often contain an array of exotic plants. The ability to predict which plants are most likely to become inva sive and which sites are most susceptible to invasion will fa cilitate efforts to prioritize the identification and control of such plants; such prioritization ultimately may be the most effective method for preventing invasions. Although the abil ity to predict which introduced species will invade a given ecosystem remains poor, the most reliable predictors of sub sequent invasion are evidence of invasiveness in other regions and whether or not the area being colonized is similar in cli mate to the invader's native range (Reichard and Hamilton 1997, Goodwin and others 1999). Disturbed areas are also ex tremely susceptible to invasion. When prioritizing plants for management, it is important to note that time lags may occur between introduction and invasion (Kowarik 1995) and that the earliest stages of an invasion are most easily and cheaply controlled. Reichard (1997) thoroughly reviews predictive techniques. Dewey and others (1991) discuss the use of re mote sensing data to predict areas susceptible to future inva sions. For more publications about the factors that affect plant invasions, see section II.B. Understanding Plant Invasions.

Chicoine, Timothy K.; Fay, Peter K.; Nielsen, Gerald A. 1985. Predicting weed migration from soil and climate maps. Weed Science. 34(1): 57 61.

Annotation: This study attempted to identify areas vulnerable to spotted knapweed (*Centaurea maculosa*) invasion by locating regions that most closely resembled the climatic and edaphic characteristics of sites previously infested. Suitable ranges of these characteristics were originally determined from 116 established infestations of spotted knapweed. No single variable effectively predicted which uninfested areas might be vulnerable to knapweed invasions. However, combinations of variables accurately identified potential sites. The authors discuss the limitations of this technique for predicting potential weed migrations, but also highlight that it is easy to use and has potential for predicting locations of other types of weeds.

Daehler, Curtis C.; Strong, Donald R. 1996. Status, prediction and prevention of introduced cordgrass *Spartina* spp. invasions in Pacific estuaries, USA. Biological Conservation. 78: 51 58.

Annotation: See section III.B. Page 35.

Dewey, Steven A.; Price, Kevin P.; Ramsey, Doug. 1991. Satellite remote sensing to predict potential distribution of dyers woad (*Isatis tinctoria*). Weed Technology. 5(3): 479 484.

Annotation: This study used data on the spectral reflectance of different landcover types taken from a satellite (Landsat 5 Thematic Mapper) to identify areas that were suitable for invasion by dyers woad (*Isatis tinctoria*), and to predict the potential distribution of this exotic plant on noninfested lands in a National Forest in Utah. Ten of 60 cover types were strongly associated with current dyers woad infestations and therefore considered suitable. If suitable areas within the National Forest were colonized by dyers woad, this would represent a 124 fold increase in its distribution. Using this approach to predict potential weed invasions over large, diverse, and inaccessible landscapes would allow land managers greater efficiency and accuracy in managing weeds. Identifying potential invasion sites might also allow control efforts to begin earlier, minimizing the spread of the target weed and the associated long term costs.

Goodwin, Brett J.; McAllister, Andrew J.; Fahrig, Lenore. 1999. Predicting invasiveness of plant species based on biological information. Conservation Biology. 13(2): 422 426.

Annotation: This study sought to determine, first, whether invasiveness of a species can be predicted from readily available biological information, and, secondly, whether invasiveness can be predicted more successfully using a species' biological attributes or using its original geographic range. The biological characteristics tested were life form, stem height, and flowering period. The authors compared 165 plants of European origin that successfully invaded New Brunswick, Canada, with the same number of European noninvasive congeners. Although the invasive and noninvasive congeners did differ significantly in two out of three biological attributes, these characters did not correctly predict invasiveness. In contrast, a species' original geographic range was an effective predictor of invasiveness. Invasive plants tended to have broader geographic ranges. This study suggests that a prediction of invasiveness on a species by species basis is not likely to diminish the accidental introduction of invasives.

Groves, R. H.; Panetta, F. D.; Virtue, J. G., eds. 2001 Weed Risk Assessment. Collingwood, Victoria, Australia: CSIRO Publishing. 244 p.

Annotation: Weed risk assessment involves predicting the invasiveness, economic and environmental impacts, and distribution of both current and potential future weeds. In addition to reviewing the concepts, examples from around the world offer predictive modeling approaches and tools for prioritizing weed species.

Hiebert, Ronald D.; Stubbendieck, James. 1993. Handbook for ranking exotic plants for management and control. U.S. National Park Service Natural Resources Rep. NPS/NRMWRO/NRR 93/08. Denver, CO. 21 p. *(Note: This document can be obtained from National Park Service, Natural Resources Publication Office, P.O. Box 25287 [WASO NPRO], Denver, CO 80225 0287 or downloaded from http://www1.nature.nps.gov/pubs/ranking.)*

Annotation: This handbook presents a ranking system developed by the National Park Service to help resource managers prioritize which exotic plants to target for control efforts. The system ranks each exotic plant in terms of the significance of current and potential impacts, the feasibility of controlling it, and the level of urgency for taking action. This ranking system allows managers to concentrate efforts and limited resources on the most disruptive and controllable plants. After discussing the components of the ranking system, the handbook provides examples from several natural areas of how to use it.

Higgins, Steven I.; Richardson, David M.; Cowling, Richard M. 2001. Validation of a spatial simulation model of a spreading alien plant population. Journal of Applied Ecology. 38: 571 584.

Annotation: Spatial simulation models are especially sensitive to which parameters, or variables, are used and what values are input for those parameters. This paper represents a rare attempt at validating a spatial model so it can be appropriately applied to management. In addition to validating the model, the authors explain the model in detail, discuss the sensitivity of model parameters, and discuss the limits of their assumptions. The spatially explicit model described is one of few existing models that estimate the spread of plant populations. The authors used field data to assign recruitment, dispersal, and mortality values for two alien species, and based their initial plant distribution on 1938 aerial photographs. Model output was then compared to invasion patterns as seen on 1989 aerial photographs. For all six study sites, the range of modeled outputs included the rates and patterns of spread evidenced on the 1989 photographs, suggesting that the model may be a valuable tool for exploring management scenarios. However, the authors noted that model predictions were better for the species with wind dispersed seeds than the species with bird dispersed seeds, because it is hard to predict where birds will deposit seeds. The use of spatially explicit models allows the incorporation of disturbance events, long distance dispersal, and propagule availability, factors that cannot be easily included in nonspatial analytical models.

Higgins, Steven I.; Richardson, David M.; Cowling, Richard M.; Trinder-Smith, Terry H. 1999. Predicting the

landscape-scale distribution of alien plants and their threat to plant diversity. Conservation Biology. 13(2): 303 313.

Annotation: The primary objectives of this paper were (1) to predict the potential distribution of alien plants in relation to several environmental variables in the Cape Peninsula of South Africa, and (2) to overlay these predictions with current dis tributions of native plants to evaluate the potential threat that these exotics pose to native biota. The authors found that most exotics threaten more native plants than might be expected, based on the area they are predicted to invade. They also found that species richness is a poor indicator of resistance to inva sion. This prediction technique may help prioritize threats from exotic species, highlight sites that need the most active man agement, and contribute to a strategy for managing invasions on a landscape scale.

Kowarik, I. 1995. Time lags in biological invasions with regard to the success and failure of alien species. In: Pysek, P.; Prach, K.; Rejmánek, M.; Wade, M., eds. Plant invasions: general aspects and special problems. Amsterdam, The Neth erlands: SPB Academic Publishing: 15 38.

Annotation: Long time lags between the introduction of a nonnative plant and its subsequent invasion indicate that spe cies currently considered low priority by managers could well become invasive in the future. Moreover, time lags make it extremely difficult to predict the likelihood of invasion for any given species. In this article, the author analyzed time lags for 184 species introduced near Brandenburg, Germany, for which adequate historical records were available. Approxi mately 10 percent of these plants eventually became invasive, but the time lag between introduction and invasion differed greatly among species, from 29 years to over 300. The au thors caution that many introduced plants may be in a time lag phase, and that even in the absence of additional introduc tions, the number of invasive species will increase. Invasion events, especially for plant species originating in more south erly climates, were also correlated with higher ambient tem peratures caused by urbanization and with increased disturbance as a result of World War II.

Lodge, David M. 1993. Biological invasions: lessons for ecology. Trends in Ecology and Evolution. 8(4): 133 137.

Annotation: In this article, Lodge reviews historical and re cent approaches to predicting invasive species. He criticizes previous attempts to classify invaders and invaded communi ties independently from each other, arguing that interactions between invaders and target ecosystems are highly specific. History and chance events affect ecosystem structure and func tion in ways that make it difficult to predict how a specific invader will interact with and impact that ecosystem. In re viewing traditional ideas about how invasions occur, the au thor argues that evidence for the importance of any single ecosystem process (for example, disturbance) or feature (for example, species diversity) in promoting invasions is equivo cal. Instead, if we are to have a better predictive ability and understanding of invasive species, research needs to focus on the interactions of target communities and invaders, and emerg ing patterns in those interactions.

Mack, Richard N. 1996. Predicting the identity and fate of plant invaders: emergent and emerging approaches. Bio logical Conservation. 78(1): 107 121.

Annotation: This paper reviews and evaluates various ap proaches for predicting the identity and fate of future invasive nonnative plants. The author ranks eight approaches, begin ning with those that have the most limitations and ending with those that are the most promising. He then highlights the strengths and weaknesses of each one. Prediction approaches include: (1) compiling species that have been weeds in their home range or elsewhere, (2) compiling traits of invading spe cies, (3) assessing invasive potential based on similar climate, (4) using mathematical models to predict potential rates of invasion, (5) experimentally manipulating plant environments in controlled growth chambers, (6) simultaneously growing congeners under field conditions (either comparing aliens or comparing a native with a congeneric alien), (7) experimen tally sowing or establishing plants beyond their current range (without manipulating the environment), and (8) experimen tally sowing plants beyond their current range (with manipu lations of field conditions). Using a combination of several approaches may be the most successful.

Panetta, F. D.; Mitchell, N. D. 1991. Homoclime analysis and the prediction of weediness. Weed Research. 31: 273 284.

Annotation: This study adds to a growing body of evidence that the invasive potential of a given plant is extremely diffi cult to predict. This study used homoclime analysis to predict the potential invasiveness of three exotic plants in New Zealand. Homoclimes are areas that possess similar climates. Homoclime analysis identifies regions at risk of invasion by species that have been invasive elsewhere by defining the physical limits to the distribution of an organism based on other geographic regions it has colonized, then searching for climatically similar regions. The authors used distributions of three nonnative plants in Australia to predict potentially suit able regions in New Zealand. Extensive geographic areas had a suitable climate for one of the plants, while only small areas were predicted to be climatically suitable for a second spe cies. A large area was deemed suitable for the third species. Although it has been present for over 100 years, the third spe cies has not become invasive in New Zealand.

Reichard, Sarah. H. 1997. Prevention of invasive plant in troductions on national and local levels. In: Luken, James O.; Thieret, John W., eds. Assessment and management of plant invasions. New York, NY: Springer Verlag: 215 227.

Annotation: This chapter reviews both current legislation enacted to prevent exotic plant invasions and methods for pre dicting which plants are likely to invade natural areas. Good predictors of invasiveness include a wide latitudinal range, a prior history of invasions, vegetative reproduction, a short ju venile period, a long fruiting period, and extended seed lon gevity. The author also emphasizes the importance of monitoring and outlines steps resource managers can take to reduce the probability of invasions at the local scale.

Reichard, Sarah Hayden; Hamilton, Clement W. 1997. Predicting invasions of woody plants introduced into North America. Conservation Biology. 11(1): 193 203.

Annotation: This paper developed two models to predict invasiveness based on structural, life history, and biogeo graphic characteristics of woody plants introduced into North America. The two models, discriminant function analysis and classification regression trees, correctly pre dicted between 76 percent and 86 percent of invasive woody plants. The authors then used the models to create a deci sion tree that allows the user to classify risk of invasive ness into three categories: low, high, and unknown. Overall, the best predictor of invasiveness was whether or not a spe cies was known to invade elsewhere in the world.

Rejmánek, Marcel; Richardson, David M. 1996. What at tributes make some plant species more invasive? Ecology. 77(6): 1655 1661.

Annotation: See section II.B.1 Page 14.

Tucker, K. C.; Richardson, D. M. 1995. An expert system for screening potentially invasive alien plants in South Af rican fynbos. Environmental Management. 44: 309 338.

Annotation: Exotic woody plants can be screened according to their invasive potential in the South African fynbos ecosys tem (mediterranean shrubland). The system consists of an interactive flow diagram that focuses on specific interactions between characteristics of the fynbos environment and bio logical attributes of plant species that are likely to be intro duced. Based on these interactions, the system classifies potential invaders as either "high risk" or "low risk." While this system is specific to the South African fynbos, the ap proach described in this paper may be applicable to other eco systems, particularly those experiencing periodic disturbances (such as fire) that result in "invasion windows" that can be exploited by exotic species.

Wadsworth, R. A.; Collingham, Y. C.; Willis, S. G.; Hunt ley, B.; Hulme, P. E. 2000. Simulating the spread and man agement of alien riparian weeds: are they out of control? Journal of Applied Ecology. 37 (Supplement 1): 28 38.

Annotation: See section III.E.1. Page 44.

D. Finding, Mapping, and Monitoring Invasive Plants

Initiating an inventory and monitoring program is a critical first step in managing exotic plants. The ability to detect, map and monitor exotic plants over large areas has improved with the advent of new technologies such as global positioning sys tems (GPS) and geographic information systems (GIS) (Lass and Callihan 1993, Prather and Callihan 1993), geostatistics (Donald 1994), and remote sensing (Everitt and others 1995, Lachowski and others 1996). Many of the following papers discuss recent developments in using such technologies for managing invasive plants. Johnson (1999) gives a recent over view of methods used to map and monitor weeds, and Stohlgren and others (1998) recommend that surveys should focus on riparian zones and other disturbed, nutrient rich areas. Additionally, Brown and others (2001) describe an ef fective volunteer monitoring program.

Benninger-Truax, Mary; Vankat, John L.; Schaefer, Rob ert L. 1992. Trail corridors as habitat and conduits for movement of plant species in Rocky Mountain National Park, Colorado, USA. Landscape Ecology. 6(4): 269 278.

Annotation: See section II.B.3. Page 22.

Brown, William T.; Krasny, Marianne E.; Schoch, Nina. 2001. Volunteer monitoring of nonindigenous invasive plant species in the Adirondack Park, New York, USA. Natural Areas Journal. 21(2): 189 196.

Annotation: Volunteer invasive plant monitoring program can be successful. Training and using volunteer monitors was shown to be an effective strategy for natural area managers with limited financial and staff resources. A road corridor sur vey was designed in order to collect data useful for manage ment and to provide volunteers with a meaningful experience so they would participate in future conservation efforts. The authors note that the survey was less a rigorous scientific tool and more a provider of good baseline invasive plant information. The data, together with volunteers' informal observation and knowledge, were used to set management and monitoring priorities. The paper details recommenda tions for others considering the adoption of a volunteer monitoring program (defining appropriate goals, designing data collection and management systems, and providing volunteer support).

Dewey, Steven A.; Price, Kevin P.; Ramsey, Doug. 1991. Satellite remote sensing to predict potential distribution of dyers woad (*Isatis tinctoria*). Weed Technology. 5: 479 484.

Annotation: See section III.C. Page 37.

Donald, William W. 1994. Geostatistics for mapping weeds, with a Canada thistle (*Cirsium arvense*) patch as a case study. Weed Science. 42(4): 648 657.

Annotation: Geostatistics is a method of mapping weed dis tributions that was originally developed for underground geo logical deposits. It uses data collected at known points within and surrounding a population then interpolates between points to create a map showing isoclines of the chosen variable. For example, measuring the density of seedlings at several known points would result in a map showing isoclines of seedling density (this is identical to how elevation is illustrated on a topographic map). In this technical paper, the authors discuss its application to monitoring a perennial weed species, Canada thistle. This method is particularly useful for mapping and si multaneously monitoring several important biological or de mographic aspects of a given weed population (in other words, densities of mature plants and seedlings, seed set, seed bank, root or shoot biomass, and so forth) over time.

Everitt, James H.; Escobar, David E.; Aleniz, Mario A.; Davis, Michael R.; Richerson, James V. 1996. Using spa tial information technologies to map Chinese tamarisk (*Tamarix chinensis*) infestations. Weed Science. 44(1): 194 201.

Annotation: Remote sensing combined with global positions system (GPS) and geographic information system (GIS) can be used to detect and map Chinese tamarisk (saltcedar; *Tamarix chinensis*) along riparian areas in the Southwestern United States. Aerial color video imagery (to determine cover esti mates) was successfully integrated with GPS (to record lati tude/longitude coordinates). Weed distribution maps can then be combined in GIS with other attribute information. These technologies can enable managers to develop maps depicting where infestations occur over large or inaccessible areas. See annotation for Everitt and others (1995) below.

Everitt, J. H.; Escobar D. E.; Davis M. R. 1995. Using remote sensing for detecting and mapping noxious plants. Weed Abstracts. 44(12): 639 649.

Annotation: This paper describes the potential of different remote sensing techniques to detect and map noxious plants on rangeland and in natural areas. The authors illustrate the pros and cons of aerial photography, airborne videography, and satellite sensor imagery, their applicability for monitoring nonnative plants, and how they were used to identify and map various weed species on rangeland in Texas. Many species were only visible during specific life stages (for example, when flowering). This emphasizes the importance of considering seasonal changes in detection probability for a given species when using remote sensing technology. Certain plant characteristics, such as their canopy architecture or leaf pubescence, also significantly affected detectability. According to the authors, combining computer analyses with remote sensing images provides a useful tool for estimating areas of noxious weed spread on rangelands, which facilitates monitoring. The remote sensing technique used depends on the user's needs, resources at hand, and the species of weed involved.

Johnson, Douglas E. 1999. Surveying, mapping, and monitoring noxious weeds on rangelands. In: Sheley, Roger L.; Petroff, Janet K., eds. Biology and management of noxious rangeland weeds. Corvallis, OR: Oregon State University Press: 19 35.

Annotation: This chapter provides a general introduction to and overview of techniques used in surveying, mapping, and monitoring invasive nonnative plants. The author first describes survey techniques ranging from opportunistic sighting reports to systematic surveys, as well as their limitations. In addition, he briefly describes quantitative methods for acquiring more detailed information about the frequency, density, aboveground phytomass, and cover of invasive plants, and shows how these parameters can be used to obtain other important indices for monitoring. Next, he outlines two large scale means of surveying and mapping exotic plant distributions and patterns of invasion: global positioning systems and remote sensing methods. Finally, he discusses the use of geographic information systems for mapping exotic plants.

Lachowski, Henry; Varner, Vicky; Maus, Paul. 1996. Noxious weeds and remote sensing: a literature review prepared for the Remote Sensing Steering Committee. Salt Lake City, UT: Remote Sensing Applications Center, U.S. Department of Agriculture, Forest Service; RSAC 2 LIT1. 10 p. (*Note: This document can be obtained by contacting the Remote Sensing Applications Center, 2222 W. 2300 South, Salt Lake City, UT 84119; 801 975 3750.*)

Annotation: This literature review begins with a brief introduction to the problem of exotic plant invasions on range lands, then discusses the benefits of remote sensing for mapping and monitoring noxious weeds, the types of remote sensing tools currently in use, and the biological characteristics of weeds that can be mapped using remote sensing methods. The authors then review studies (up to 1996) using remote sensing technology for mapping and monitoring weeds. Some have detected weeds based on their unique life stage or spectral characteristics, while others combine remote sensing data with geographic information systems to narrow the scope of data collection to only those habitats likely to contain the target weed species. The bibliography includes 22 references.

Lake, Leonard; Anderson, Bruce; Varner, Vicky; Lachowski, Henry. 1997. Mapping and monitoring noxious weeds using remote sensing. Range management: remote sensing tips. RSAC 7140 2. Salt Lake City, UT: Remote Sensing Applications Center, U.S. Department of Agriculture, Forest Service. 4 p. (*Note: This document can be obtained by contacting the Remote Sensing Applications Center, 2222 W. 2300 South, Salt Lake City, UT 84119; 801 975 3750.*)

Annotation: This study tested the feasibility of using several types of remote sensing imagery to detect and map four exotic plant species (yellow starthistle [*Centaurea solstitialis*], spotted knapweed [*Centaurea maculosa*], leafy spurge [*Euphorbia esula*], and rush skeletonweed [*Chondrilla juncea*]) in central Idaho. The authors discuss the benefits and drawbacks of images taken by 70 mm and 35 mm camera, color infrared digital camera, and multispectral video cameras. Field validations revealed that while areas of extensive weed growth were easily detected, many low density weed areas were not discernible. The timing of data collection was the most critical factor influencing their ability to distinguish noxious weeds from the surrounding cover types. Because some plants are more visible from the air when flowering, while others are best detected during other phenological stages, managers monitoring multiple weed species may need to conduct more than one remote sensing flight. For example, leafy spurge was discernible on all aerial imagery, whereas rush skeletonweed, while present, was not detected by any method due to a lack of distinctive visible characters when the images were taken. Despite its limitations, remote sensing may be an extremely useful tool in efforts to control weeds by establishing a baseline for monitoring. This will in turn, facilitate predictions of future weed spread and the planning and evaluation of weed control programs.

Lass, Lawrence W.; Callihan, Robert H. 1993. GPS and GIS for weed surveys and management. Weed Technology. 7(1): 249 254.

Annotation: Global positioning system (GPS) technology is often used in conjunction with geographic information systems (GIS) for surveying exotic plants, but questions exist as to the accuracy and feasibility of the technology. Such technology may not only expedite surveying and mapping of nonnative plants, but also may facilitate overall management of weed infestations. The authors compare estimates of the boundaries of a common crupina (*Crupina vulgaris*) infestation determined using GPS to boundaries estimated by field crews using topographic maps and transferred to GIS by digitization. GPS is more accurate in determining the infestation boundaries. An additional advantage of GPS is its ability to interface with GIS to accurately position weed infestations in relation to other recognizable physiographic map features such as wilderness boundaries, trails, roads, and streams. The authors conclude that despite certain limitations, GPS is precise enough for mapping weed infestations that it will greatly aid weed management efforts.

Marcus, W. Andrew; Milner, Gary; Maxwell, Bruce. 1998. Spotted knapweed distribution in stock camps and trails of the Selway-Bitterroot Wilderness. Great Basin Naturalist. 58(2): 156 166.

Annotation: See section II.B.3. Page 23.

Prather, Timothy S.; Callihan, Robert H. 1993. Weed eradication using geographic information systems. Weed Tech nology. 7(1): 265 269.

Annotation: Geographic information systems (GIS) are use ful for control programs for nonnative plants. In addition to providing a database for recordkeeping, GIS can be used to plan control strategies, determine control costs, and monitor remediation efforts. Specific uses of GIS include highlighting areas to be surveyed, determining the size of infestations, de lineating areas sensitive to control measures, and tracking particular control efforts. The authors illustrate the usefulness of GIS in eradication programs using a case study of a control program for common crupina (*Crupina vulgaris*).

Self, David W. 1986. Exotic plant inventory, rating, and management planning for Point Reyes National Seashore. In: Thomas, Jr., L. K., ed. Proceedings: conference on science in the National Parks, 1986, Vol. 5: Management of exotic species in natural communities; 1986 July 13 18; Fort Collins, CO. U.S. National Park Service and The George Wright Soci ety: 85 95.

Annotation: This paper describes an exotic plant inventory conducted on the Point Reyes National Seashore, California. Plant introductions combined with intense grazing pressure have severely altered the character of both wilderness and nonwilderness lands. Each of the 190 species identified in the field survey were rated for their ecosystem impact, visual im pact, population size, number of sites, and likelihood of in crease under different conditions. Based on these ratings, the authors developed priority rankings. Forty one species were recommended as high priority for control, and maps and con trol methods were developed for these species. Almost all of the 77 problem species were expected to increase without action. Recommendations for exotic plant management are briefly listed, including the use of fire and native grass restoration.

Stohlgren, Thomas J.; Bull, Kelly A.; Otsuki, Yuka; Villa, Cynthia A.; Lee, Michelle. 1998. Riparian zones as havens for exotic plant species in the central grasslands. Plant Ecol ogy. 138: 113 125.

Annotation: See section II.B.2. Page 21.

Zamora, David L.; Thill, Donald C. 1999. Early detection and eradication of new weed infestations. In: Sheley, Roger L.; Petroff, Janet K., eds. Biology and management of nox ious rangeland weeds. Corvallis, OR: Oregon State Univer sity Press: 73 84.

Annotation: This chapter outlines and discusses important considerations in the detection and eradication of nonnative plant infestations. According to the authors, for eradication efforts to be successful, a noxious weed management plan must incorporate ways of detecting new invaders before they be come fully established. An eradication plan should consider the population dynamics of a plant (life cycle, seed bank, spread) and tailor treatments to specific locations that the tar get species has invaded. The authors also elaborate on the com ponents of an effective eradication strategy: locating and prioritizing treatment areas, adopting a treatment schedule, imposing quarantine measures, revegetating, conducting ap praisal surveys, and estimating costs.

E. Control and Eradication

The control and eradication of invasive plants is a rapidly expanding discipline, yet the effectiveness of various control methods remains an important research need. Historically, control efforts have focused on manual or mechanical removal, burning, and poorly regulated biological control. Herbicides later succeeded these as the favored method of control, but increasing concern about their impact on the environment and public health has led to an era of integrated control using mul tiple techniques. The current focus of invasive plant control is shifting toward prevention, early detection, target specific herbicides, low impact removal techniques, regulated testing and release of biocontrol agents, and nontoxic biopesticides. Papers in these sections provide information for determining which species to prioritize and factors to consider when se lecting control methods.

In the first section, Randall (1996) and Heibert (1997) de scribe strategies for prioritizing invasive plants to control, and Heibert and Stubbendieck (1993) and Randall and others (2001) provide practical ranking systems for prioritizing spe cies. Several authors (Mullin 1992, Sheley and others 1999a) discuss integrated weed management, and Ashton (1989) and Pieterse and Murphy (1990) review the control of invasive aquatic plants. The biocontrol section includes DeLoach's (1997) review of the concepts underlying biological control, Follett and Duan's (2000) review of nontarget effects, examples of nontarget impacts by biocontrols (Harris 1988, Howarth 1991, Louda and others 1997, Pearson and others 2000, and Blossey and others 2001) and concepts and tools for assessing the likelihood of nontarget effects prior to release (Louda 1998, Pemberton 2000, Schaffner 2001). Papers in the chemical con trol section explain how herbicides work (Bussan and Dyer 1999), investigate the effects of herbicides on native plant and animal species (Marrs and Lowday 1984, Mayes and others 1987, Bedunah and Carpenter 1989, Hitchmough and others 1994, Rice and others 1997b, Tyser and others 1998, Litt and others 2001) and natural processes (Baker and Mickelson 1994), and include discussions that help readers decide when to use chemical control techniques (Tu and others 2001) and when to apply them to minimize nontarget effects (Hitchmough and others 1994, Rice and others 1997b, Rice and Toney 1998). The final section addresses fire (Post and others 1990, Bock and Bock 1992, Hastings and DiTomaso 1996, Keeley 2001) and grazing (Thomsen and others 1993, Germano and others 2001, Tu and others 2001) as control strategies.

1. Developing and Prioritizing Control Strategies

Alien Plants Ranking System, [Online]. Available: http://usgssrv1.usgs.nau.edu/swepic/aprs/ranking.html [2002, July 31].

Annotation: See annotation in section IV.B.2. Page 57.

Anderson, Bruce; Wotring, Ken. 2001. Invasive plant man agement along wild rivers: are we stewards, guardians, or gardeners? International Journal of Wilderness. 7(1): 25 29.

Annotation: This article describes the process by which a stew ardship team within the USDA Forest Service is addressing the problem of invasive weeds along the Salmon River in the Frank Church River of No Return Wilderness (FCRNRW), Idaho. Through research and public involvement within the FCRNRW, the interests and concerns of wilderness user groups were assessed. A strong majority of public comments on nox ious weed management within the FCRNRW supported ag gressive weed management to restore ecosystems. The team agreed on an approach based on this sentiment, and they have extensively involved various wilderness users (individuals and groups) and private landowners in their management plan. This article details the development, implementation, and future intentions of this restoration program. The ability of the team to establish priorities at the wilderness scale rather than by land ownership or administrative management unit was noted.

Ashton, Peter. J.; Mitchell, David. S. 1989. Aquatic plants: patterns and modes of invasion, attributes of invading species and assessment of control programmes. In: Drake, J. A.; Mooney, H. A.; di Castri, F.; Groves, R. H.; Kruger, F. J.; Rejmánek, M.; Williamson, M., eds. Biological invasions: a global perspective. Chichester, England: John Wiley and Sons: 111 154.

Annotation: See section II.B.1. Page 13.

Colton, T. F.; and Alpert, P. 1998. Lack of public awareness of biological invasions by plants. Natural Areas Jour nal. 18(3): 262 266.

Annotation: Public involvement is necessary if biological invasions are to be controlled, yet little information is avail able about public perceptions of plant invasions. The authors examined the public's knowledge of biological invasions by surveying people who visited the Bodega Marine Laboratory in northern California. Most respondents were relatively well educated but showed limited familiarity with the concepts of biological invasion and biological diversity. Similarly, the term "weed" was used mostly as it related to a backyard nuisance, allergies, and a plant that was prickly or injurious. Weeds were thought of as invasive but not necessarily nonnative, and those that cause serious problems for public agencies were rarely mentioned. Moreover, few people thought weeds caused seri ous ecological or economic impacts, and a minority supported additional efforts to control weeds. Nevertheless, the public appeared open to education. Managers and administrators of control programs may want to educate the public in a context of personal experience by publicizing cases of biological in vasions in the regions where the control programs are taking place.

Exotic Plant Management Teams, [Online]. Available: http://www.nature.nps.gov/epmt [2002, July 31].

Annotation: The National Park Service developed the con cept of Exotic Plant Management Teams (EPMT) to combat exotic plant species. Each team provides highly trained plant management specialists to assist parks with limited resources in controlling infestations before it becomes impossible or prohibitively expensive to do so. Teams are adaptable to dif ferent regions and employ the expertise and capabilities of local citizens and agencies. Currently, four teams are operat ing: Pacific Islands EPMT, Florida Partnership EPMT, Chihuahuan Desert/Southern Shortgrass Prairie EPMT, and National Capital Region EPMT. Six additional teams were identified for development in fiscal year 2002.

Fuller, T. C.; Barbe, G. Douglas. 1985. The Bradley method of eliminating exotic plants from natural reserves. Fremontia. 13(2): 24 25.

Annotation: See section III.E.4. Page 50.

Groves, Richard H. 1989. Ecological control of invasive terrestrial plants. In: Drake, J. A.; Mooney, H. A.; di Castri, F.; Groves, R. H.; Kruger, F. J.; Rejmánek, M.; Williamson, M., eds. Biological invasion: a global perspective. Chichester, England: John Wiley and Sons: 437 462.

Annotation: The author reviews control methods and emplasizes the importance of using a combination of pre vention, mechanical/manual control, fire, chemical control, competition with native plants, and biological control. He also suggests timing controls to coincide with critical stages in the reproductive cycle of the target plant. Finally, he outlines four principles of invasive plant control in nature reserves: (1) integrated control is more effective than any single method by itself, (2) control methods that add diver sity to the ecosystem are more successful than those that simplify it, (3) control must be a long term effort, and (4) control efforts must be adequately monitored and evalu ated.

Groves, R. H.; Panetta, F. D.; Virtue, J. G., eds. 2001. Weed Risk Assessment. Collingwood, Victoria, Australia: CSIRO Publishing. 244 p.

Annotation: See section III.C. Page 37.

Hiebert, Ronald D. 1997. Prioritizing invasive plants and planning for management. In: Luken, James O.; Thieret, John W., eds. Assessment and management of plant invasions. New York, NY: Springer Verlag: 195 212.

Annotation: See section III.A. Page 33.

Hiebert, Ronald D.; Stubbendieck, James. 1993. Handbook for ranking exotic plants for management and control. U.S. National Park Service Natural Resources Rep. NPS/NRMWRO/NRR 93/08. Denver, CO. 21 p. (*Note: This document can be downloaded from http://www1.nature.nps.gov/pubs/ranking or obtained from Pub lications Coordinator, National Park Service, Natural Re sources Publication Office, P.O. Box 25287 [WASO NPRO], Denver, CO 80225 0287.*)

Annotation: See section III.C. Page 37.

Hoshovsky, Marc C.; Randall, John M. 2000. Management of invasive plant species. In: Brossard, Carla C.; Randall, John M.; Hoshovsky, Marc C., eds. Invasive plants of California's wildlands. University of California Press: Berke ley, CA: 19 27.

Annotation: While most of the book consists of information about the biology and control of California's invasive nonna tive species, this readable chapter provides an overview of control strategies and methods that might be used in parks, preserves, and other wildlands throughout the United States. The chapter begins by describing an adaptive management approach that includes defining management goals and objec tives, determining which species or populations are most likely to block management objectives, identifying available weed control methods, implementing a management plan to move toward goals and objectives, monitoring the outcome of management actions, and refining goals and objectives. The authors provide insight into setting control priorities, they comment on unintended adverse effects of herbicide, biocontrol, and manual control methods, and they underscore the importance of preventing new invasions over controlling weeds that are already established and widespread. The remainder of the chapter is a thorough and clearly written review of knowledge related to physical, biological, and chemical control methods including techniques to minimize the risk of unintended and harmful side effects.

Madsen, John D. 1997. Methods for management of nonindigenous aquatic plants. In: Luken, James O.; Thieret, John W., eds. Assessment and management of plant invasions. New York, NY: Springer Verlag: 145 171.

Annotation: See section III.A. Page 33.

Moody, Michael E.; Mack, Richard N. 1988. Controlling the spread of plant invasions: the importance of nascent foci. Journal of Applied Ecology. 25: 1009 1019.

Annotation: This study used model simulations to evaluate the effectiveness of different control strategies on the spread of an invading terrestrial plant. The authors compared the area occupied by an initial population composed of a single large expanding focus to the area occupied by newly established and spreading satellite foci under varying control regimens. Control strategies included reducing the area of the main focus, destroying some satellites, or combinations of both strategies. Controlling even 30 percent of the satellites greatly improved the effectiveness of control measures. Any apparent gain from a substantial reduction in the area of the main focus was soon offset by the proliferation and eventual growth of smaller satellites. This remained true even when the initial area of the main focus was 10,000 fold greater than that of the satellite population (in other words, nascent focus) and the population initially had no satellites. These results suggest that the current practice of controlling large or conspicuous infestations at the expense of eradicating small isolated populations may have little effect in the long term reduction of invasive plants. Managers will improve the success of control programs by locating and eliminating satellite populations.

Mullin, Barbra. 1992. Meeting the invasion: integrated weed management. Western Wildlands. 18: 33 38.

Annotation: This paper describes an approach to the management of nonnative exotic plants called integrated weed management (IWM). IWM attempts to use the most appropriate control techniques for a target weed species in a planned, coordinated program designed to limit the plant's impact and spread. The author touches on various methods of managing and controlling exotic plants, including prevention, education, physical and mechanical control, biological control, chemical control, cultural control, and land management, and emphasizes the importance of cooperative local planning efforts. She then outlines the goals and accomplishments of the Western Weed Coordinating Committee and presents a hypothetical example of the way local landowners can work together to control weeds.

Pieterse, Arnold H.; Murphy, Kevin J., eds. 1990. Aquatic weeds: the ecology and management of nuisance aquatic vegetation. Oxford, UK: Oxford University Press. 593 p.

Annotation: This text compiles much of the existing information on the biology, ecology, and control of aquatic plants. The chapters are divided into the (1) concepts, characteristics, and ecology of aquatic weeds; (2) aquatic weed management (in other words, control); and (3) important aquatic weed problems and their management in different regions of the world. This text generally focuses on "the world's most troublesome aquatic weeds." It includes chapters on physical and chemical control methods, as well as the use of biological control agents, such as insects, fungal pathogens, and plant eating fish. The authors also include a chapter on the harvesting and economic uses of aquatic weeds.

Prather, Timothy S.; Callihan, Robert H. 1993. Weed eradication using geographic information systems. Weed Technology. 7(1): 265 269.

Annotation: See section III.D. Page 41.

Randall, John M. 1993. Exotic weeds in North American and Hawaiian natural areas: The Nature Conservancy's plan of attack. In: McKnight, Bill N., ed. Biological pollution: the control and impact of invasive exotic species. Indianapolis, IN: Indiana Academy of Science: 159 172.

Annotation: This paper reviews the nonnative plant control strategy and activities of The Nature Conservancy (TNC), a nonprofit organization that operates the largest system of privately owned reserves in the world. The author discusses TNC's creation of a national level invasive weed specialist position to coordinate weed control efforts and the dissemination of information on nonnative species in the form of Element Stewardship Abstracts. In addition, the author presents examples of control efforts on a number of TNC preserves. TNC managers strive to view the control or eradication of invasive plants as one aspect of an overall ecosystem restoration effort. After establishing priorities and goals for weed control, managers use mechanical, chemical, and/or biological control methods. In certain cases, weed problems are addressed via restoration of natural fire or hydrologic regimes and by reintroducing native species.

Randall, John M. 1996. Weed control for the preservation of biological diversity. Weed Technology. 10(2): 370 383.

Annotation: See section I. Page 7.

Randall, John M. 1997. Defining weeds of natural areas. In: Luken, James O.; Thieret, John W., eds. Assessment and management of plant invasions. New York, NY: Springer Verlag: 18 25.

Annotation: See section II.A. Page 12.

Randall, J. M.; Benton, N.; Morse, L. E. 2001. Categorizing invasive plants: the challenge of rating the weeds already in California. In Groves, R. H.; Panetta, F. D.; Virtue, J. G. (eds.) Weed Risk Assessment. Collingwood, Victoria, Australia: CSIRO Publishing: 203 216.

Annotation: Using California as an example, this publication presents a practical ranking system that can be used to determine the overall priorities of wildland weed species for research and control at State, regional, or national levels. This ranking system uses objective and clear criteria related to species' impacts on wildlands and native plant habitats, biological characteristics and dispersal abilities, distribution and abundance in the United States, and management potential.

The "Wildland Weed Priority Rank Form" is included as an appendix. The final step on this form is to calculate overall priority ranks that represent the significance of each species' threat to native species and native plant habitat in the United States.

Schmitz, D. C.; Schardt, J. D.; Leslie, A. J.; Dray, Jr., F. A.; Osborne, J. A.; Nelson, B. V. 1993. The ecological impact and management history of three invasive alien aquatic plant species in Florida. In: McKnight, Bill N., ed. Biological pollution: the control and impact of invasive exotic species. Indianapolis, IN: Indiana Academy of Science: 173 194.

Annotation: See section II.C.1. Page 27.

Schmitz, Don C.; Simberloff, Daniel. 2001. Biological invasions: a growing threat. Issues in Science and Technology. 13: 33 40.

Annotation: See section III.B. Page 36.

Schwartz, Mark W.; Randall, John M. 1995. Valuing natural areas and controlling nonindigenous plants. Natural Areas Journal. 15(2): 98 100.

Annotation: See section III.A. Page 34.

Sheley, Roger L.; Kedzie-Webb, Susan; Maxwell, Bruce D. 1999b. Integrated weed management on rangeland. In: Sheley, Roger L.; Petroff, Janet K., eds. Biology and management of noxious rangeland weeds. Corvallis, OR: Oregon State University Press: 57 68.

Annotation: This chapter describes the various phases of an integrated weed management program. The first phase consists of education, inventory, and impact assessment. The second includes prioritizing weed problems, and choosing and implementing management techniques for target areas. The third phase involves adopting proper grazing management practices, while the fourth phase consists of evaluating the management approach and techniques, and making necessary adjustments to fit desired goals. Because integrated weed management should be founded on ecologically sound principles, the authors also present two models that can be used to direct data collection, assemble and process information, and predict the outcome of various combinations of control measures. First, the successional rangeland weed management model can be used to guide the integration of various control methods by manipulating the three components of succession (disturbance, colonization, and species performance). Second, the life history model predicts the outcome of various integrated weed management strategies based on the life history traits of a weed population and demographic processes.

Tu, Mandy; Hurd, Callie; Randall, John M. 2001. Weed control methods handbook. The Nature Conservancy, Version: April 2001. (*Note: This document is available online at http://tncweeds.ucdavis.edu/handbook.html.*)

Annotation: The handbook begins with a discussion of adaptive management and recommends a strategy for formulating weed control programs. The subsequent chapters describe specific control methods: manual and mechanical removal, grazing, prescribed fire, biological control, with detailed information on 10 herbicides that have been used in natural areas. The advantages and disadvantages of each method are discussed, sometimes in regard to specific species, and examples of successful and unsuccessful use of each method are included. Tools and techniques are also described and recommended. They also discuss the use of different methods in conjunction with each other. The handbook includes abundant information on herbicides, but the authors stress that all available control options should be considered when formulating a weed control program.

Wadsworth, R. A.; Collingham, Y. C.; Willis, S. G.; Huntley, B.; Hulme, P. E. 2000. Simulating the spread and management of alien riparian weeds: are they out of control? Journal of Applied Ecology. 37 (Supplement 1): 28 38.

Annotation: By modeling the spread of two invasive riparian species across heterogeneous landscapes, the authors assessed six control strategies. The six alternative strategies prioritized large population size, old populations, new populations, upstream populations, populations near urban areas, or random populations; there was also a "no control" strategy. They evaluated treatment intensity (area treated per year), treatment efficiency (proportion of plants destroyed), and time of treatment after population establishment, and they assessed the effectiveness of these alternative strategies on controlling weeds in individual catchments versus the entire region. Prioritizing treatments based on population size and spatial distribution (in other words, near urban areas or upstream) were the most effective strategies, rather than age of population or random. Relatively high intensities and efficiencies were needed for successful control, especially for the species that had a faster rate of spread. They conclude that controlling large populations, which are the principal source of propagules, may be the most efficient strategy for species that exhibit long distance dispersal; whereas first eradicating small outlying populations (for instance, see Moody and Mack 1988) may be more effective for species with short range dispersal events. In addition to describing the relevance of this exercise, the authors explain how the model works, what they used for parameters, and which parameters were most sensitive for each of the species modeled.

Westman, Walter E. 1990. Park management of exotic plant species: problems and issues. Conservation Biology. 4(3): 251 260.

Annotation: See section III.F. Page 54.

Whelan, Christopher J.; Dilger, Michael L. 1992. Invasive, exotic shrubs: a paradox for natural area managers? Natural Areas Journal. 12(2): 109 110.

Annotation: See section III.F. Page 54.

Zamora, David L.; Thill, Donald C. 1999. Early detection and eradication of new weed infestations. In: Sheley, Roger L.; Petroff, Janet K., eds. Biology and management of noxious rangeland weeds. Corvallis, OR: Oregon State University Press: 73 84.

Annotation: See section III.D. Page 41.

Zamora, David L.; Thill, Donald C.; Eplee, Robert E. 1989. An eradication plan for plant invasions. Weed Technology. 3(1): 2 12.

Annotation: For both ecological and economic reasons, complete eradication of invasive plants before they become ubiquitous is better than having to conduct long term control efforts. The authors present a generalized scheme for how to plan and initiate eradication efforts, including considerations for early detection, assessing noxious status, surveying and monitoring, modeling population dynamics to assess the level of threat, and eradication technologies and strategies. Nevertheless, the authors acknowledge the limitations of this approach when dealing with large, persistent infestations and emphasize that adequate funding for comprehensive eradication plans and action at the local level are necessary to successfully prevent the spread of invasive plants.

Zavaleta, Erika. 2000. The economic value of controlling an invasive shrub. Ambios. 29 (8): 462 467.

Annotation: In this study, the author evaluated the economic impacts of tamarisk (salt cedar, *Tamarix* spp.), an invasive shrub of arid and semiarid riparian areas in the Western United States. She assessed how the invasion of tamarisk has impacted two natural ecosystem functions (water availability and flood protection), tallied the cost associated with these impacts, and compared that to the cost of a regional removal and restoration campaign. Though conservative estimates of the cost of tamarisk eradication and riparian restoration were high, complete recovery of such costs was projected to occur in as few as 17 years. These figures do not include societal or ecological benefits of tamarisk removal that, along with the economic benefits, would continue long into the future. Zavaleta argues that, at times when funding is limited and social and ecological arguments alone are not convincing enough to fund conservation, economic measures associated with restoring ecosystems can provide crucial catalysts for management actions. This case study provides an excellent example of the benefits of invasive species control and native restoration efforts.

2. Biological Control

Blossey, Bernd; Casagrande, Richard; Tewksbury, Lisa; Landis, Douglas A.; Wiedenmann, Robert N.; Ellis, Donna R. 2001. Nontarget feeding of leaf-beetles introduced to control purple loosestrife (*Lythrum salicaria* L.). Natural Areas Journal. 21: 368 377.

Annotation: The authors offer a general discussion of the nontarget effects of biological controls, and focus specifically on the feeding and breeding habits of leaf beetles introduced in an attempt to control purple loosestrife. They conduct a host specificity test to determine the possibility of the introduced beetles feeding on plants other than loosestrife. In no choice feeding tests, the beetles did eat certain other species. However, their life cycle could only be completed on loosestrife. The authors refer to this phenomenon as "spillover" rather than host shifting, and argue that such nontarget feeding only occurs when the control agents' populations increase rapidly or other food sources are scarce. The authors conclude that host specificity tests are the best way to assess potential adverse effects of biological control agents, and that most nontarget feeding events are transient.

Briese, D. T. 1996. Biological control of weeds and fire management in protected nature areas: are they compatible strategies? Biological Conservation. 77(2 3): 135 141.

Annotation: See section II.B.2. Page 15.

DeLoach, C. Jack. 1997. Biological control of weeds in the United States and Canada. In: Luken, James O.; Thieret, John W., eds. Assessment and management of plant invasions. New York, NY: Springer Verlag: 172 194.

Annotation: This book chapter starts with an overview of the concepts underlying biological control and the methods used to implement it. This is followed by case studies that high light the community level ecological benefits of control programs. The author describes protocols for each stage of a biocontrol research program. He then reviews biological control efforts for major classes of weeds in the United States and Canada by region, and concludes with an overview of future directions and research needs. Progress needs to be made in four main areas: (1) preventing the importation of additional nonindigenous species, (2) improving the success rate of biocontrol programs, (3) expanding the scope of exploratory surveys for new biocontrols, and (4) increasing public under standing of exotic plant impacts to provide public support for biocontrol programs.

Follett, Peter A.; Duan, Jian J. 2000. Nontarget effects of biological control. Boston, MA: Kluwer Academic Publishers: 316 p.

Annotation: The outcome of a symposium at the 1997 annual meeting of the Entomological Society of America, this book synthesizes and represents diverse viewpoints related to nontarget effects of biological controls. The first section re views the debate between those concerned about possible host shifting and practitioners of classical biological controls, discusses what constitutes a "nontarget," investigates the frequency and strength of nontarget effects, and examines the impact of nontarget concerns on the practice of biological control. The rest of the book highlights nontarget issues by re viewing examples of past nontarget effects while controlling parasitoids and predators, weeds, or pathogens.

Gassmann, A.; Louda, S. M. 2001. *Rhinocyllus conicus*: initial evaluation and subsequent ecological impacts in North America. In: Wajnberg, E.; Scott, J. K.; Quimby, P. C., eds. Evaluating indirect ecological effects of biological control. CAB International: 147 167.

Annotation: The recent evaluation of direct and indirect ecological effects of the flowerhead weevil, *Rhinocyllus conicus* Fröl., in North America has partially stimulated a renewed debate over the risk of nontarget effects in biological control. *R. conicus* was released for control of true thistles (*Cirsium* spp.) but is increasing in population and exhibiting host range expansion. This is having a significant impact on native North American plant and insect species. The authors reviewed the published data for *R. conicus*. They examined its host plant interactions in Europe before, and during the 15 years after, its release in North America to determine the extent to which host range expansion and associated ecological effects on native North American species were predicted or predictable. Following their review, the authors came to three important points. First, the potential effect of *R. conicus* on native North American species was not a major element of the testing program. Second, the prerelease and the early postrelease data did suggest the probability of host range expansion of *R. conicus* on multiple North American *Cirsium* species and was therefore predictable, yet this evidence was discounted. Third, a clear prediction of the ecological consequences of *R. conicus* feeding on native North American *Cirsium* was not possible because the quantification of the probable magnitude of that feeding was not done. They conclude that there was sufficient data to have warranted further testing to define and quantify the potential ecological side effects of introducing *R. conicus* to North America.

Harris, P. 1988. Environmental impact of weed-control insects. BioScience. 38(8): 542 548.

Annotation: This article reviews the unintended ecological impacts of biological controls on nontarget plants using case studies of St. Johnswort, *Hypericum perforatum*, in the Western United States and ornamental lantana, *Lantana camara*, in Uganda. Two documented situations in which biocontrol insects have directly and significantly impacted nontarget plants are: (1) when low densities of the target species leads to host shifting in biocontrols; and (2) when selection for increased survival occurs on abundant, closely related nontarget species. For a variety of reasons, biocontrols are unlikely to significantly affect populations of rare plants.

Howarth, Francis G. 1991. Environmental impacts of classical biological control. Annual Review of Entomology. 36: 485 509.

Annotation: Biological controls often have unintended, negative effects on the environment that generally have been overlooked. This landmark review discusses the broader environmental impacts of introducing biological controls and factors that influence whether a biocontrol will have a detrimental effect on native species. Howarth uses case studies to illustrate various negative impacts of biocontrol introductions as well as the ecological mechanisms underlying them. Negative impacts include a wide variety of native species extinctions and population declines. Direct risks to nontarget organisms depend on several factors, including (1) the persistence of the introduced control species, (2) the range of the host species and the habitats it can utilize, (3) the potential for shifting to a native host, (4) whether rapid changes in the biocontrol's genotype or morphology can occur, (5) the biocontrol's behavioral flexibility, and (6) the "vulnerability" of the ecosystem into which it is introduced. Islands, freshwater habitats, and tropical regions are particularly vulnerable to negative effects from introduced biocontrols. The author then discusses case studies in which biocontrol species have lead to public health problems, major economic losses, and social conflicts between groups that place different values on the species being controlled. The risk from unauthorized introductions and the release of novel, genetically engineered organisms is also briefly reviewed. An important first step in reducing the detrimental effects of biocontrols is simply recognition of the problem among biologists, land managers, and the general public. Improved regulatory restrictions and more research into nontarget effects prior to introductions are also needed.

Louda, Svata M. 1998. Ecology of interactions needed in biological control practice and policy. Bulletin of the British Ecological Society. 29(4): 8 11.

Annotation: In light of recent evidence of detrimental ecological impacts from nonnative biocontrol agents, the author re examines the controversy over their appropriate use and makes specific suggestions for improving current biocontrol practices and policies. Because the introduction of biocontrol agents in a new ecosystem is irreversible, the ecological and economic threat of target species should be carefully assessed and alternative control measures (for example, chemical, manual, native biocontrols) considered before their release. Louda also argues that additional research into the ecological side effects of biocontrol agents should be incorporated into the prerelease testing process. Because of the potential for widespread impacts, ecologists and other stakeholders need to assume a more prominent role in the decisionmaking process regarding releases of biocontrols.

Louda, S. M.; Kendall, D.; Connor, J.; Simberloff, D. 1997. Ecological effects of an insect introduced for the biological control of weeds. Science. 277: 1088 1090; 22 August.

Annotation: Monitoring the ecological consequences of biocontrol introductions is a relatively new and important area of research. In this paper, the authors demonstrate the direct and indirect ecological impacts of an introduced biocontrol insect on native species. Twenty years after its release in the Western United States, a flowerhead weevil introduced to control invasive musk thistle (*Carduus* spp.) and its relatives subsequently colonized three species of native thistles (*Cirsium* spp.) in nearby National Parks. In Rocky Mountain National Park, weevil populations grew exponentially and significantly reduced the reproductive success of native thistles. As the abundance of weevil larvae in the seedheads of native thistles increased, the numbers of native thistle herbivores also declined. The authors challenge the conventional expectation that there is little environmental risk with the release of biological agents for weed control, and they underscore the need for rigorous, ecologically focused prerelease testing and postrelease monitoring of biocontrol species.

Mortensen, K. 1986. Biological control of weeds with plant pathogens. Canadian Journal of Plant Pathology. 8: 229 231.

Annotation: The author briefly reviews the use of classic biological control (introducing self perpetuating enemies of the target weed) with plant pathogens as well as the use of microbial pesticides (mainly herbicides) in agricultural settings. The former method is usually better suited to invasive plants on rangeland and in natural areas, while the latter is often used in lieu of chemical herbicides on cropland. Limitations of each approach are discussed, including restrictions due to cost and marketability.

Pearson, Dean E.; McKelvey, Kevin S.; Ruggiero, Leonard F. 2000. Nontarget effects of an introduced biological control agent on deer mouse ecology. Oecologia. 122: 121 128.

Annotation: This paper provides an example of the cascading nontarget effects of an otherwise "safe" introduced biological control agent. Although nonnative species greatly affect the ecosystems they invade, biological control agents introduced to curb the spread of invasive species can also have unintended ecological effects. This study examines the ecological impact of *Urophora* gall flies introduced to control spotted knapweed, *Centaurea maculosa*, on a native, nontarget species, the deer mouse, *Peromyscus maniculatus*. Since the introduction of the biocontrol agent, deer mice have seasonally shifted their diet and habitat use away from native grassland to take advantage of abundant fly larvae in areas of dense knapweed infestations during the winter, spring, and early summer months. Opportunistic predation by deer mice and other predators may reduce gall fly abundance below levels needed for effective biocontrol of knapweed.

Pemberton, Robert W. 2000. Predictable risk to native plants in weed biological control. Oecologia. 125: 489 494.

Annotation: The author of this paper collected and analyzed known cases where introduced biological control agents successfully completed their life cycles on native, nontarget plant species. The author compared the degree of nontarget plant use resulting from biocontrol releases on target weeds with close relatives in the area of introduction to biocontrol releases on target weeds without close relatives in this area. The analysis was based on 117 natural enemies (112 insects, three fungi, one mite, and one nematode) established on 55 weed species in the continental United States, Caribbean, and Hawaii between 1902 and 1994. Fifteen introduced insect species adopted 41 native plants as hosts, and all but one plant were closely related to the target weeds or to plants used by the insects in their native areas. Only one of the 117 agents used an unpredicted host plant, and this single case may not have resulted in a persistent host relationship. Based on these data, the author concludes that nontarget plant use can be reliably predicted prior to the introduction of agents. He concludes that native plant use can be avoided or greatly minimized by targeting weeds with fewer native plant relatives and by introducing agents with suitably narrow diets.

Schaffner, Urs. 2001. Host range testing of insects for biological control: how can it be better interpreted? BioScience. 51: 951 959.

Annotation: The deliberate release of biological agents to control invasive plants has usually been considered environmentally safe. Host range testing, however, has often resulted in ambiguous results, and at least two species released to control exotic plants have switched to closely related native species (*Rhinocyllus conicus* feeding on native *Cirsium* species and *Tyria jacobaeae* on native arrowleaf ragwort [*Senecio triangularis* Hook]). The ambiguity has resulted from test designs that required considerable interpretation. Theoretical evolutionary biologists and ecologists have gained valuable insight into host specificity and the underlying genetic processes. Indeed, the author discusses several examples where results from indepth studies on the behavior and genetics of a biocontrol candidate may contribute to the interpretation of screening tests (for example, the acceptance of native and exotic *Potentilla* by *Tinthia myrmosaeformis* moths). Therefore, collaboration between applied and theoretical ecologists can drastically improve the evaluation of prerelease studies. Schaffner also includes a glossary of terms relevant to biological control and theoretical ecology.

Sheldon, Sallie P.; Creed, Jr., Robert P. 1995. Use of a native insect as a biological control for an introduced weed. Ecological Applications. 5(4): 1122 1132.

Annotation: The authors examined the suitability of a native weevil to act as a biocontrol for an introduced, invasive aquatic plant. The native weevil (*Euhrychiopsis lecontei*) substantially reduced the biomass of introduced Eurasian watermilfoil (*Myriophyllum spicatum*) in both field and lab experiments, but did not have any detrimental effects on nontarget native species (other than its natural host, a native milfoil). This study demonstrates that the use of native biocontrols is a feasible, ecologically less risky, and economically less expensive alternative for controlling unwanted invasive plants.

Simberloff, Daniel; Stiling, Peter. 1996. Risks of species introduced for biological control. Biological Conservation. 78: 185 192.

Annotation: Biological control is often touted as an environmentally friendly alternative to herbicides, but numerous cases exist where biocontrols have negatively affected nontarget species. Although many of the impacts on nontarget species resulted form releases in the earliest years of using them, ecosystems and communities are complex and don't necessarily follow the simplified interactions represented by host specificity tests. Moreover, proposals have surfaced to introduce biological controls to control unwanted native species, as part of a "neoclassical biological control program." As a result, the authors urge managers and regulators considering the use of biological controls to perform cost benefit analyses. Although some invasions are likely to be catastrophic and affect entire communities, the implications of introducing other living organisms as biocontrols should also be considered. Despite the absence of conclusive evidence that rapid evolution of biocontrols has become problematic, the risks exist. Indeed, only a small proportion of the world's taxa are actually observable, and the complex interactions of ecosystem processes are only beginning to be identified, let alone understood. The authors argue that additional research and rigorous testing is necessary despite the costs, and the United States should strive to carefully construct laws that allow biological control while reducing the likelihood of unintended damage.

Stelljes, Kathryn B.; Wood, Marcia. 2000. Foreign agents imported for weed control. Agricultural Research. 48: 4 9; March.

Annotation: This popular article highlights current research on biological controls by the U.S. Department of Agriculture, Agricultural Research Service's (ARS) Weed Science program. It gives an overview of ARS organization, facilities, and their cooperative programs with the Animal and Plant Health Inspection Service, and illustrates their activities using case studies of their existing biological control programs.

Story, Jim M. 1992. Biological control of weeds: selective, economical and safe. Western Wildlands. 18(2): 18 23.

Annotation: This popular article reviews the historical background and concepts behind biological control programs and strongly promotes their use as an integral part of noxious weed management plans. Focusing on Montana, the history and status of biocontrol programs prior to the article's publication date are reviewed and summarized in a table that includes spotted and diffuse knapweed, leafy spurge, musk, Canada and Russian thistles, dalmation toadflax, and St. Johnswort.

Strobel, Gary A. 1991. Biological control of weeds. Scientific American. 265(1): 72 78.

Annotation: Biological control of unwanted exotic plants may be a cost efficient and environmentally safe alternative to applying chemical pesticides. In this popular article, Strobel reviews traditional biocontrol approaches using insects or pathogens, as well as recent progress in developing species specific phytotoxins, also known as bioherbicides, derived from pathogens.

U.S. Department of Agriculture. 2000. Reviewer's manual for the technical advisory group for biological control agents of weeds: guidelines for evaluating the safety of candidate biological control agents. U.S. Department of Agriculture, Animal and Plant Health Inspection Service, Plant Protection and Quarantine. 212 p. *(Note: This document is available online at http://www.aphis.usda.gov/ppq/permits/tag/tag.pdf.)*

Annotation: These guidelines are intended to provide information about the Technical Advisory Group for Biological Control Agents of Weeds as well as technical information useful in reviewing and evaluating petitions for biological control releases. In addition, the guidelines present an overview of biological control agents (both insects and pathogens), with sections on identification and characteristics, and testing for host specificity. The manual also includes numerous appendices, including agency perspectives on using biological controls, suggested formats for petitions and test plant lists, a comprehensive reference list, plant classification, a list of weeds for which agents have been released, and an example of an environmental assessment for biological control agents. The intent is to facilitate information sharing among those interested in evaluating biological control agents, and assisting the review, evaluation, and approval processes within the USDA.

Wapshere, A. J. 1974. A strategy for evaluating the safety of organisms for biological weed control. Annals of Applied Biology. 77: 201 211.

Annotation: In the past, biological control agents were tested using the crop testing method: each important crop was exposed to the biocontrol to determine whether damage to that crop would result. Broader, more rigorous "biologically relevant tests" were proposed in later years. Wapshere suggested using a phylogenetic method, combining crop testing with biologically meaningful tests. His proposal began with the centrifugal phylogenic testing method, which involved exposing the biocontrol to a series of plants that were successively more distantly related to the proposed host than the previous set. As a safeguard, he suggested a second set of tests that examined cultivated plants (because agricultural weeds were often the targets of early biocontrol). The author believed the strategy would effectively separate somewhat polyphagous (feeding on a relatively diverse number of plants) organisms from monophagous (usually feeding on one plant) or oligophagous (generally feeding on one plant genus or family) organisms. Moreover, the strategy was particularly effective at determining the safety of organisms such as rusts and gall makers. The phylogenetic strategy presented by Wapshere was based on a current understanding of behavioral and physiological ecology that accounted for the morphological and biochemical similarities of plants. Nevertheless, discoveries more recent than this paper, including insight into the genetics underlying insect behavior and evolution, emphasize the need for cautious interpretation of host specificity tests (see Schaffner 2001 in section III.E.2 page 47).

Wilson, Linda M.; McCaffrey, Joseph P. 1999. Biological control of noxious rangeland weeds. In: Sheley, Roger L.; Petroff, Janet K., eds. Biology and management of noxious rangeland weeds. Corvallis, OR: Oregon State University Press: 97 115.

Annotation: Biological control of weeds has become one of the primary methods of controlling naturalized exotic plants (those that are widespread and cannot be eradicated). This chapter provides a thorough review of how biological controls work, which types of organisms are used, and considerations for developing a biological control program. The authors also discuss several recent developments in the field, including issues of ecological risks, nontarget effects, conflicts of interest, and the "biological control treadmill" effect, in which successful control of target species leads to their replacement by other, nonnative plants.

3. Chemical Control

Baker, James L.; Mickelson, Steven K. 1994. Application technology and best management practices for minimizing herbicide runoff. Weed Technology. 8: 862 869.

Annotation: Major characteristics of herbicides that determine their fate include soil adsorption and persistence. If an herbicide is categorized as strongly adsorbed, it persists mostly in soil sediments. If it is moderately adsorbed, it is removed by surface runoff, and if it is categorized as weakly or nonadsorbed, it leaves the soil through percolation. Persistence refers to how long the herbicide remains in the soil and is related to its breakdown, solubility, adsorption, and its vapor pressure. Adsorption and persistence are influenced by soil properties such as the amount of organic and clay content and pH, and environmental conditions such as temperature and soil water content. Runoff loss is directly related to the herbicide concentration, but the method and timing of application are also factors. Herbicides interact with the soil and rainfall in a 1 cm thick layer of soil called the mixing zone, and carefully planned application can reduce the potential losses to runoff. Managers should also consider that washoff from vegetation residue may return herbicides to the system even with small amounts of rain. Baker and Mickelson focus mainly on the interaction of herbicides and agricultural practices; however, much of the application technology is directly relevant to natural systems.

Bedunah, Don; Carpenter, Jeff. 1989. Plant community response following spotted knapweed (*Centaurea maculosa*) control on three elk winter ranges in western Montana. In: Fay, Peter K.; Lacey, John R., eds. Proceedings: knapweed symposium; 1989 April 4 5; Bozeman, MT. Extension Bulletin 45. Bozeman, MT: Montana State University: 205 212.

Annotation: This study examined the effect of different herbicide control treatments for spotted knapweed on three elk winter range sites. Knapweed sites were treated with different rates of either Clopyralid or Tordon. All herbicide treatments were effective at controlling knapweed, though after four growing seasons only the two heaviest application rates of Tordon maintained adequate control. The standing crop and seed head production of native grasses was significantly greater on all treated sites compared to nontreated sites. Grass vigor was also greater on treated sites. Native forb diversity did not decrease significantly following herbicide treatments. Studies have shown that elk show a preference for grasses. Controlling knapweed will therefore improve the condition of elk winter range by promoting the growth and vigor of native grasses.

Bussan, Alvin J.; Dyer, William E. 1999. Herbicides and rangeland. In: Sheley, Roger L.; Petroff, Janet K., eds. Biol ogy and management of noxious rangeland weeds. Corvallis, OR: Oregon State University Press: 116 132.

Annotation: This chapter is designed to help managers select the appropriate herbicide for a specific weed management plan. It explains how herbicides kill plants, how they are applied, and how they interact with the environment. The authors first discuss aspects of herbicide application (formulations, carri ers, spray additives, spray gallonage and timing, and herbi cide labels), and the way in which plants take up and absorb herbicides (root uptake, foliar uptake, translocation, metabolic interactions). Next, the authors provide a more detailed de scription of the various types of rangeland herbicides. After a brief discussion of herbicide resistant weeds, the authors then discuss the interaction of herbicides with the environment (plant uptake, soil herbicide interactions, off target move ment). Throughout, the authors emphasize that herbicides are most successful at controlling weeds when they are incorpo rated into a long term integrated weed management plan.

Fay, Pete. 1992. The role of herbicides in weed management. Western Wildlands. 18(2): 24 26.

Annotation: After a brief description of how various herbi cides work, the author touches on some of the positive and negative aspects of using herbicides to control weeds. Using three case studies of invasive weeds in Montana, the author then shows that the role of herbicides in a weed management program depends on both the target weed species and the se verity of the invasion.

Hitchmough, J. D.; Kilgour, R. A.; Morgan, J. W.; Shears, I. G. 1994. Efficacy of some grass specific herbicides in controlling exotic grass seedlings in native grassy vegeta tion. Plant Protection Quarterly. 9(1): 28 34.

Annotation: A series of experiments helped evaluate the effi cacy of several grass specific herbicides at removing exotic grass seedlings growing among native grasses. The herbicides showed no marked selectivity between native and exotic seed lings in greenhouse trials. However, herbicides did control mature exotic plants, while native plants survived the treat ments. Under seminatural conditions, weed seedlings were killed, while native grasses showed regrowth after initial die back. The authors suggest that managers: (1) base their deci sion to control weeds on an objective assessment of the exotic plant(s)' capacity to disrupt the native community, (2) time herbicide applications in relation to the growth physiology of the native grasses to minimize impacts on the native commu nity, and (3) ensure that "resistant" species and other types of exotics are not unintentionally encouraged by applying herbi cides.

Litt, Andrea R.; Herring, Brenda J.; Provencher, Louis. 2001. Herbicide effects on ground-layer vegetation in south ern pinelands: a review. Natural Areas Journal. 21(2): 177 188.

Annotation: The authors conducted a literature review to ex amine the effects of widely used herbicides on ground layer vegetation in Southern pinelands. Of the 125 studies exam ined via specific criteria, only 21 were worthy of review. The majority of these were conducted on pine plantations, but also included studies in sandhills (communities on xeric sand ridges with high pines) and flatwoods (communities on poorly drained, acidic sandy soils with open pine forests). Due in part to the variety of herbicides used and the diversity of re sponses that were measured, few commonalities were revealed. Woody plant cover generally declined with herbicide use, but effects on herbaceous plant cover were mixed. Most studies documented a decrease in total woody and herbaceous plant species richness and a decline in species of special concern. They conclude that widespread use of herbicides, either to reduce hardwood encroachment or to control weeds, in South ern pinelands may have undesirable effects on nontarget plant species and recommend additional studies be conducted be fore treating large, diverse landscapes. The authors were troubled by the small number of studies designed to assess herbicidal effects in these environments and the lack of ex perimental rigor and inconsistent reporting standards among studies.

Marrs, R. H.; Lowday, J. E. 1984. Herbicidal control of weeds on nature reserves with special reference to lowland heaths. Institute for Terrestrial Ecology Annual Report. 1983: 30 35.

Annotation: After briefly discussing the problems associated with herbicide use on nature reserves, the authors describe an experiment that tested the effects of nine herbicide treatments on nontarget vegetation, and they provide detailed compari sons of treatment options for two invasive plant species in Great Britain, nonnative birch (*Betula* spp.) and bracken fern (*Pteridium aquilinium*). For broad spectrum herbicides, they recommend choosing direct application methods that mini mize nontarget effects.

Mayes, M. A.; Hopkins, D. L.; Dill, D. C. 1987. Toxicity of picloram (4-amina-3,5,6-trichloropicolini acid) to life stages of the rainbow trout. Bulletin of Environmental Contamina tion and Toxicology. 38: 653 660.

Annotation: This study was conducted to evaluate the effects of exposure to picloram on fish populations. Picloram is used to control broad leaf and woody plants. Embryo larval and acute tests were conducted on rainbow trout, measuring mor tality, growth rates, and other sublethal effects at differing lev els of exposure. At certain concentrations, the authors found reduced growth rates. However, they conclude that under use guidelines in effect at the time of publication, picloram does not constitute an acute or chronic threat to aquatic life.

Rice, Peter M.; Toney, J. Christopher. 1998. Exotic weed control treatments for conservation of fescue grasslands in Montana. Biological Conservation. 85: 83 95.

Annotation: Herbicides are often used to control exotic knap weed (*Centaurea maculosa*) infestations in native grasslands in Montana. The authors outline a framework for analyzing the most important effects of herbicides, including: (1) the effectiveness of various herbicide treatment levels and timing of application for controlling knapweed, (2) changes in simi larity to exemplary native communities, (3) the impacts on and resilience of native species, and (4) subsequent changes in community structure. Results suggest that native commu nities in earlier invasion stages are more resilient to and ben efit more from herbicide applications. Some native plant species were more sensitive to common herbicide applications than others. Herbicide applications should be timed around the phenology of native plant reproduction so as to minimize

impacts during their primary growing season; in western Mon
tana, late summer or fall applications may be best.

Rice, Peter M.; Toney, J. Christopher; Bedunah, Donald J.; Carlson, Clinton E. 1997b. Plant community diversity and growth form responses to herbicide applications for control of *Centaurea maculosa*. Journal of Applied Ecology. 34: 1397 1412.

Annotation: This study examined the effects of various her bicide treatments for controlling knapweed (*Centaurea maculosa*) on the structure and species diversity in native grass lands in Montana. Herbicides effectively reduced knapweed on the study plots. Initial declines in native plant abundance and diversity were no longer apparent by the third year fol lowing the treatments. The authors recommend applying her bicides in the autumn, which is after the sensitive growth period for most native plant species. Planning the rate, frequency, and timing of herbicide applications is important for reducing impacts on native species.

Suszkiw, Jan. 2000. Fungal protein slows broadleaf weeds. Agricultural Research. 48(2): 10 11.

Annotation: Biopesticides are emerging as a new, nontoxic alternative to chemical pesticides. This review article describes new research into biopesticides aimed at controlling invasive broadleaf weeds. When applied to leaves, proteins derived from the fungus *Fusarium oxysporum* induce a hypersensitive de fense mechanism in plants that rapidly kills leaf cells, leads to leaf wilting and death, and reduces plant survival and repro duction. The protein breaks down relatively quickly in the environment and is thought to be harmless to nontarget or ganisms. Biopesticides may be a new option for safely man aging weeds in wilderness.

Tu, Mandy; Hurd, Callie; Randall, John M. 2001. Weed control methods handbook. The Nature Conservancy, Ver sion: April 2001. (*Note: This document is available online at http://tncweeds.ucdavis.edu/handbook.html.*)

Annotation: The fifth chapter, Guidelines for Herbicide Use, is designed to help readers carefully consider the impacts of herbicide use on conservation targets, other native species, and the rest of the ecological system. It also addresses the health and safety of applicators and others in the vicinity, and includes a checklist summarizing the steps needed to ensure that adequate consideration has been given to whether the use of herbicides is warranted for each individual case. See full annotation in section III.E.1. Page 44.

Tyser, Robin W.; Asebrook, Jennifer M.; Potter, Rachel W.; Kurth, Laurie L. 1998. Roadside revegetation in Gla cier National Park, U.S.A.: effects of herbicide and seed ing treatments. Restoration Ecology. 6(2): 197 206.

Annotation: Roads often promote the establishment and spread of nonnative plants into nature reserves by increasing soil disturbance and eliminating existing native plants along roadsides. The authors evaluated the effectiveness of various seeding regimes and herbicide treatments in restoring native fescue prairie along roads in Glacier National Park. Broad casting native grass seeds increased the proportion of native grasses. The use of herbicides increased native grasses and decreased alien forbs, but spraying also increased nonnative grasses and reduced native forbs. The authors caution that res

toration is a difficult and complex process, but make several recommendations for improvements. They suggest establish ing dense, low diversity, disturbance resistant, native plant cover (for example, rhizomatous grasses) along roadsides, in creasing monitoring of alien plants, and assessing the amount of alien and native seeds in the soil.

Williams, T. 1997. Killer Weeds. Audubon. March April: 24 31.

Annotation: Williams' popular article examines a difficult, yet common dilemma faced by Western natural areas manag ers how to control invading weeds in the face of insufficient government funds, conflicting demands from user groups, and legal opposition from environmental organizations. The ar ticle takes a look at the legal and ecological impacts of a 1984 injunction against herbicide use on USDA Forest Service and USDI Bureau of Land Management lands in Oregon and Wash ington. Managers argue that the 5 year injunction on herbi cide use allowed previously small and isolated populations of invasive weeds to become established and spread widely on managed Federal lands. The selective use of herbicides as part of an integrated weed management plan may be one of the few viable options for controlling the early stages of an inva sion, a time during which eradication is still possible. The author presents examples of successful weed management programs, concluding that the environmental community should reconsider the costs and benefits of using herbicides, and work with, rather than against, Federal agencies to create an effective program for invasive species control.

4. Mechanical and Manual Control

Fuller, T. C.; Barbe, G. Douglas. 1985. The Bradley method of eliminating exotic plants from natural reserves. Fremontia. 13(2): 24 25.

Annotation: This paper outlines a simple control strategy for small reserves containing exotics that can be controlled through hand pulling. The four step hand pulling plan consists first of preventing the deterioration of the least infested area; second, eliminating weeds where the native vegetation abuts a mix ture of weeds and natives; progressing slowly to allow regen erating natives to stabilize each cleared area; and finally, making inroads into areas composed almost entirely of non native species.

McCarthy, Brian C. 1997. Response of a forest understory community to experimental removal of an invasive nonindigenous plant (*Alliaria petiolata*, Brassicaceae). In: Luken, James O.; Thieret, John W., eds. Assessment and Man agement of Plant Invasions. New York, NY: Springer Verlag: 117 130.

Annotation: The author experimentally tested the effects of introduced garlic mustard on a floodplain understory plant community and the efficacy of hand weeding as a control measure. Comparisons of cover and species composition on weeded treatment plots versus unmanipulated control plots suggest that weeding garlic mustard results in a temporary proliferation of native annuals, herbaceous and woody vines, and tree seedlings. However, perennial herbs, grasses, sedges, and small shrubs showed no differences in response between control and treatment plots, but this may be due to latent inhi bition (in other words, residual allelopathy) or because plant responses were not detectable during the short duration of the study (three growing seasons). The author suggests that regular bouts of hand weeding may give native plants a "release" period from competition that, in the long run, may be less harmful to the ecosystem than attempting widespread control or eradication efforts using mechanical, biological, or chemical means. Weeding appears to be an effective control method for garlic mustard but is only logistically feasible for small, colonizing populations.

Tu, Mandy; Hurd, Callie; Randall, John M. 2001. Weed control methods handbook. The Nature Conservancy, Version: April 2001. (*Note: This document is available online at http://tncweeds.ucdavis.edu/handbook.html.*)

Annotation: The first chapter, Manual and Mechanical Control Techniques, describes how to implement a variety of manual techniques while minimizing site disturbance and the transfer of weeds. They also describe several innovative manual control tools. See full annotation in section III.E.1. Page 44.

5. Other Control Methods: Fire and Grazing

Bock, J. H.; Bock, C. E. 1992. Vegetation responses to wildfire in native versus exotic Arizona grassland. Journal of Vegetation Science. 3: 439 446.

Annotation: This study compared the impacts of fire on native versus exotic grassland communities in Arizona to determine whether fire facilitates the recovery of native vegetation in sites dominated by exotic African lovegrass. The native and exotic grasslands were equally tolerant of fire. This probably resulted from both native and exotic grasses having evolved in fire adapted ecosystems. Based on this study, the authors conclude that fire is an ineffective tool for restoring native flora to sites dominated by African lovegrasses.

Germano, David J.; Rathbun, Galen B.; Saslaw, Larry R. 2001. Managing exotic grasses and conserving declining species. Wildlife Society Bulletin. 29(2): 551 559.

Annotation: Exotic annual grasses have become the dominant vegetation in many habitats in California's San Joaquin Valley. The authors maintain that plants and animals native to the area are adapted to relatively open desert habitats, and the dense exotic grass cover is having a negative effect on their survival. They conclude that the best method to control exotic grasses is through the use of livestock. Although livestock overgrazing is often responsible for the initial invasion of exotic plants, they say that discontinuing grazing rarely allows native vegetation to reestablish itself. If properly used, grazing can be used to reduce nonnative vegetation density, thereby allowing natives to gain a foothold. While the authors feel that grazing is the most important tool available to combat exotic grasses, they also list the potential problems with this approach and make it clear that this use of livestock must be closely managed, allowing for flexibility in the extent and intensity of grazing to respond to plant growth and climatic conditions.

Hastings, Marla S.; DiTomaso, Joseph M. 1996. Fire controls yellow star thistle in California grasslands: test plots at Sugarloaf State Park. Restoration and Management Notes. 14(2):124 128.

Annotation: This article describes an ongoing and successful project to control yellow star thistle (*Centaurea solstitialis*) in a northern California grasslands that historically experienced fire (6 to 20 year fire frequency). A management program of annual burns led to a dramatic decrease in mature thistles, seedlings, and the seed bank compared to those in a control area. Multiyear burns were necessary to decrease the seed bank, and this control strategy was superior to other techniques. The timing of the burn (after native grasses cured and set seed and before the thistle seed matured) was critical. The researchers found that patchy fire intensity was not problematic, but burning during the appropriate stage of plant development was important. Planting annual grasses prior to the burn may be necessary to allow for sufficient fuels to carry the fire. The researchers documented an increase in the abundance and diversity of native plant species following these burns. Although this management program also includes herbicide use and mechanical control near facilities, roadsides, and areas without sufficient fuels, burning is the preferred management action.

Keeley, Jon E. 2001. Fire and invasive species in Mediterranean-climate ecosystems of California. In: Galley, Krista E. M.; Wilson, Tyrone P., eds. Proceedings of the invasive species workshop: the role of fire in the control and spread of invasive species. Fire Conference 2000: The First National Congress on Fire Ecology, Prevention, and Management. Misc. Pub. No. 11, Tall Timbers Research Station, Tallahassee, FL: 81 94.

Annotation: See section II.B.2. Page 18.

Lacey, John R.; Wallander, Rosie; Olson-Rutz, Kathrin. 1992. Recovery, germinability, and viability of leafy spurge (*Euphorbia esula*) seeds ingested by sheep and goats. Weed Technology. 6(3): 599 602.

Annotation: Because sheep and goats consume many nonnative plants, they have been used as biological controls. The objective of this study was to quantify the role of sheep and goats as disseminators of leafy spurge (*Euphorbia esula*) seeds. Four sheep and four goats were fed spurge seeds in a controlled setting, and results indicated that digestion destroyed most but not all seeds. Goats passed all seeds by day 5, and although it took sheep 9 days to pass all seeds, most were recovered by day 4. Mean seed viability decreased after ingestion relative to the control (sheep: 14 percent; goats: 31 percent; control: 90 percent), and mean germinability also decreased (sheep: 2 percent; goats: 16 percent; control: 72 percent). Although ingestion by sheep and goats effectively reduced seed viability and its ability to germinate, the authors recommend waiting 5 days after grazing leafy spurge before moving these animals onto spurge free areas.

Olson, Bret E. 1999b. Grazing and weeds. In: Sheley, Roger L.; Petroff, Janet K., eds. Biology and management of noxious rangeland weeds. Oregon State University Press, Corvallis: 85 96.

Annotation: The author relates the spread of many weeds in North America to two major factors: inherent preferences of grazing and browsing ungulates, and plant community succession. In Western North America, native plant species are at a disadvantage in competing for water and nutrients because cattle, the dominant grazer in this system, selectively graze native grasses and have low impact on nonindigenous grasses and weeds. By persistently grazing on native grasses, while avoiding shrubs and forbs, cattle have caused many rangeland ecosystems to retrogress from a climax state of plant community succession. The author recommends restoring a balance to these disturbed systems through the introduction or reintroduction of small ruminants, such as sheep, that pre fer nonindigenous forbs. Sheep grazing applies pressure to the forbs within a plant community resulting in succession toward a climax stage. The author states that within the frame work of livestock grazing and weeds, different levels of weed infestation necessitate three management strategies: preven tion, minimizing the spread of weeds, and controlling weed infestations. In this chapter the author suggests that manage ment strategies address the causes, rather than the symptoms, of weed infestations. Proper grazing management can be used to minimize the spread of certain weeds and to control large weed infestations rather than using herbicides, which are not always cost effective and which tend to address only the symp toms. Weed control techniques that incorporate the reintroduc tion of small ruminants to many Western systems, while properly managing large ungulates, will help restore balance to the eco system and will also begin to address the cause of the problem.

Post, Thomas W.; McCloskey, Elizabeth; Klick, Kenneth F. 1990. Glossy buckthorn resists control by burning (Indiana). Restoration and Management Notes. 8: 52 53. Abstract.

Annotation: This abstract outlines the results of a study test ing whether fire was an effective management tool for con trolling exotic glossy buckthorn (*Rhamnus frangula*). One year after a fall burn, number of *Rhamnus* stems increased by 48 percent. A second spring burn led to even greater increases (59 percent) in the number of *Rhamnus* stems. Although con trolled burning prevented this shrub from flowering and set ting seed, it did not diminish its ability to resprout.

Thomsen, Craig D.; Williams, William A.; Vayssiéres, Marc; Bell, Fremont. L.; George, Melvin R. 1993. Controlled grazing on annual grassland decreases yellow starthistle. California Agriculture. 47(6): 36 40.

Annotation: This study examined the effect of cattle, sheep, and goat grazing on yellow starthistle (*Centaurea solstitialis*). Grazing in the bolting stage in late spring and early summer reduced the starthistle canopy, seed production, and thatch accumulation, and enhanced native plant diversity. Most starthistle plants were able to regrow and flower after an ini tial grazing, so close monitoring and regrazing before spines appeared on the plants were essential. Cattle, sheep, and goats differed in their acceptance of starthistle. Repeated grazing during starthistle's most vulnerable growth period can effec tively manage infestations, but additional control measures are needed to further reduce starthistle populations.

Tu, Mandy; Hurd, Callie; Randall, John M. 2001. Weed control methods handbook. The Nature Conservancy, Ver sion: April 2001. (*Note: This document is available online at http://tncweeds.ucdavis.edu/handbook.html*.)

Annotation: The second chapter of this handbook synthesizes information about and presents resources for using grazing as a control method. The third chapter addresses prescribed burning as a method for controlling invasive plants. Each chap ter includes examples of the technique's application. See full annotation in section III.E.1. Page 44.

Wallander, Roseann T.; Olson, Bret E.; Lacey, John R. 1995. Spotted knapweed seed viability after passing through sheep and mule deer. Journal of Range Manage ment. 48(2): 145 149.

Annotation: To assess spotted knapweed (*Centaurea maculosa*) viability after animal ingestion, sheep and mule deer were pulse dosed with knapweed seeds. The researchers recovered 11 percent of the seeds from mule deer and 4 per cent from sheep. Viability was highly variable (0 to 26 per cent) and was generally lower than compared to seeds that were not ingested (88 to 98 percent). The majority of the seeds (over 80 percent) were excreted within 5 days. Overall, the authors conclude that sheep and mule deer can ingest, trans port, and disseminate viable knapweed seeds, and they rec ommend managers confine sheep for at least 7 days after grazing in infested areas to permit viable seeds to pass.

F. Restoration

Restoration of native species and ecosystem processes is an essential part of all control programs for invasive plants. Once an invasive plant has been removed or eradicated, the reestab lishment of native plants plays an important role in prevent ing subsequent invasions, restoring natural disturbance regimes, and restoring populations of native wildlife. Reviews of restoration approaches and concepts are found in Westman (1990) and Berger (1993). Other authors present case studies (Rosen 1982, Barrows 1993). Wilson (1989) emphasizes the importance of restoring areas with native plants, rather than with additional introduced species. Whelan and Dilger (1992) caution that complete elimination of exotic shrubs in areas where few or no native shrubs are present could lead to de clines in local populations of native songbirds; they present a more gradual approach to controlling nonnative shrubs. Fi nally, Morrison (1997) offers insight into developing well de signed restoration monitoring studies.

Barrows, Cameron W. 1993. Tamarisk control. II. A suc cess story. Restoration and Management Notes. 11(1): 35 38.

Annotation: This paper documents the restoration of a large desert riparian area that had been heavily invaded by tamarisk (*Tamarix ramosissima*). The author first describes a success ful tamarisk removal program in this California preserve. He then discusses site recovery and restoration efforts, and touches on the problem of characterizing the native biota in order to define restoration goals. He recommends compiling histori cal species lists, then bringing these species together and man aging for natural processes. In this case, recovery was quick and inexpensive because natural processes and species asso ciations were still relatively intact. Water flow returned to the area, the historic plant species composition reestablished it self, and much of the associated wildlife reoccupied the re stored habitat. Based on the impressive recovery of this area, the author concludes that tamarisk can be controlled and native vegetation restored in some situations at a reason able cost.

Berger, John J. 1993. Ecological restoration and nonindigenous plant species: a review. Restoration Ecology. 1: 74 82.

Annotation: After briefly discussing the factors that make certain species good colonizers and certain ecosystems vulnerable to invasion, the author identifies instances when restoration might successfully control invaders. In addition, he discusses manipulating hydroperiod, photoperiod, thermoperiod, edaphic conditions, and biological control agents as restoration techniques for controlling nonindigenous species. Finally, Berger provides examples of successful elimination of exotics and restoration of natives using fire, flooding, herbicides, manual removal, shading, and substrate removal in conjunction with restoration efforts.

Cione, Nancy K.; Padgett, Pamela E.; Allen, Edith B. 2002. Restoration of a native shrubland impacted by exotic grasses, frequent fire, and nitrogen deposition in southern California. Restoration Ecology. 10(2): 376 384.

Annotation: The native coastal sage scrub system has been overrun with exotic grasses, a result of fragmentation, grazing, altered fire regimes, and the changes in nutrient availability associated with disturbances. Restoration in this system required an understanding of the processes that caused the destruction or degradation and knowledge of techniques most likely to be effective. The authors examined several techniques, including mulching, hand cultivating, and herbicides, to remove the annual grasses (for example, wild oats [*Avena fatua*]) that had become prevalent in a small 62 ha park. Each treatment was replicated 10 times, five with and five without seeding. Hand cultivation and herbicides were effective at removing cover, but not a single native shrub seedling was discovered in unseeded plots. In an accidental fire, all grass and the seeded shrub seedlings were killed in treatments that had been mulched or just seeded (in other words, where cover from exotic grasses had not been removed). Shrub seedlings in areas treated with hand cultivation or herbicides were not killed, however. The authors believed the combination of cover removal and successful shrub establishment might reduce the fire return interval and restore the coastal sage scrub ecosystem.

Jacobs, James S.; Carpinelli, Michael F.; Sheley, Roger L. 1999. Revegetating noxious weed-infested rangeland. In: Sheley, Roger L.; Petroff, Janet K., eds. Biology and management of noxious rangeland weeds. Corvallis, OR: Oregon State University Press: 133 141.

Annotation: The introduction and establishment of competitive plants is essential to the successful management of weed invasions and the restoration of desired plant communities. This paper outlines methods for revegetating weed infested areas. The authors briefly describe various seeding methods, herbicides, selection of plant species to be seeded, seeding rates, seed treatments, and followup management.

Morrison, Michael L. 1997. Experimental design for exotic plant removal and restoration. In: Luken J. O.; Thieret, J. W., eds. Assessment and management of plant invasions. New York, NY: Springer Verlag: 104 116.

Annotation: This paper outlines the basic principles of experimental design necessary to research community changes resulting from plant invasions, treatment effects on target plants, and community responses after treatments to remove target plants. The author first reviews the scientific method, emphasizes the importance of developing a well designed monitoring study, and then discusses methods of sampling design and statistical analysis relevant to any study on the assessment and management of plant invasions. In addition, he provides a decision key for selecting the appropriate design for a particular study.

Rosen, Aaron. 1982. Feasibility study: eradication of kudzu with herbicides and revegetation with native tree species in two National Parks. Atlanta, GA: National Park Service Research/Resource Management Report SER 59. 59 p.

Annotation: This study had two primary objectives: (1) to test methods of eradicating kudzu (*Pueraria lobata*) from a given area using two types of herbicides, and (2) to determine an effective regime for revegetating the treated areas with native tree species before achieving 100 percent eradication. Rosen treated study plots either with a foliar uptake herbicide (Roundup), a root uptake herbicide (Velpar), or both herbicides sequentially. Roundup was applied at different seasons to test different application strategies. Velpar was found to be ineffective. Late season applications of Roundup appeared to be more effective than early season applications. Between 80 and 100 percent control was achieved in one growing season. Sites were revegetated with three native tree species. The author addressed a variety of hypotheses by planting these species under different regimes: with or without mulch and with or without seeded cover. The mulch had a limited effect on suppressing kudzu and on enhancing seedling survival. The use of annual ryegrass as a seeded cover had a negative effect on seedling survival and outcompeted natural herb cover. All three native tree species showed good early survival, ranging from 82 to 95 percent in the two parks.

Roundy, Bruce A.; McArthur, E. Durant; Haley, Jennifer S.; Mann, David K., comps. 1995. Proceedings: wildland shrub and arid land restoration symposium. 1993 October 19-21; Las Vegas, NV. Gen. Tech. Rep. INT GTR 315. Ogden, UT: U.S. Department of Agriculture, Forest Service, Intermountain Research Station. 384 p.

Annotation: This publication is a compilation of papers from a symposium on wildland shrub and arid land restoration. The proceedings emphasize the use of revegetation in the rehabilitation of arid and semiarid lands. Contributed papers range from general overviews of the restoration of arid lands to more specific papers on arid land plant ecology. A few papers discuss the complexities inherent in trying to manage lands invaded by exotics (for example, "Restoration ecology: limits and possibilities in arid and semiarid lands," by E. B. Allen, and "Implications of early Intermountain range and watershed restoration practices," by S. B. Monsen and E. D. McArthur), while one addresses the restoration of invaded areas more directly ("Replacing Lehmann lovegrass [*Eragrostis lehmanniana*] with native grasses," by S. H. Biedenbender and others).

Sher, Anna A.; Marshall, Diane E.; Gilbert, Steven A. 2000. Competition between native *Populus deltoids* and invasive *Tamarix ramosissima* and the implications for reestablishing flooding disturbance. Conservation Biology. 14(6): 1744 1754.

Annotation: Disturbance regime and competitive ability are two important factors affecting the dynamics of invasive and native species abundances. Reintroduction of flooding is being promoted as a tool for restoring cottonwood (*Populus deltoids*), but flooding can also encourage the invasive saltcedar (*Tamarix ramosissima*). The authors examine whether restoring the disturbance regime will be an effective management tool based on the competitive ability of cottonwood and saltcedar seedlings. Certainly, cottonwood seedlings were competitively superior to those of saltcedar, but this relationship does not mean cottonwood can outcompete established saltcedar. In fact, saltcedar may exclude cottonwood establishment where natural disturbance regimes have already been reduced through human intervention. Therefore, management to restore this system may require some initial removal of existing vegetation before reestablishing a disturbance regime that mimics historical disturbance in this system.

Tyser, Robin W.; Asebrook, Jennifer M.; Potter, Rachel W.; Kurth, Laurie L. 1998. Roadside revegetation in Glacier National Park, U.S.A.: effects of herbicide and seeding treatments. Restoration Ecology. 6(2): 197 206.

Annotation: See section III.E.3. Page 50.

Walker, Lawrence R.; Smith, Stanley D. 1997. Impacts of invasive plants on community and ecosystem properties. In: Luken, James O.; Thieret, John W., eds. Assessment and Management of Plant Invasions. New York, NY: Springer Verlag: 69 86.

Annotation: See section II.C.1. Page 28.

Westman, Walter E. 1990. Park management of exotic plant species: problems and issues. Conservation Biology. 4(3): 251 260.

Annotation: This paper explores potential problems that arise as preserve managers attempt to restore invaded plant communities in parks. Constrained by limited funding, managers sometimes focus first on the most easily controlled species. Such choices could lead to parks becoming populated by more resistant exotics. Removal of nonnative plants can also result in significant perturbations to natural ecosystems during the transition back to native cover. Westman illustrates the potential dangers inherent in controlling exotic plants and the necessity of predetermining the potential impacts of removal measures on park resources with a case study of *Eucalyptus* removal in a California park. Finally, the author recommends setting priorities for exotic species management based on the current and future ecological roles of a species in relation to existing natives, rather than solely its status as a native or a nonnative species, when evaluating its potential impact.

Whelan, Christopher J.; Dilger, Michael L. 1992. Invasive, exotic shrubs: a paradox for natural area managers? Natural Areas Journal. 12(2): 109 110.

Annotation: Invasive, exotic shrubs are often used as nest sites by native songbirds. The authors caution that if few or no native species are present (as is the case in many small, fragmented woodlots), complete elimination of these exotic shrubs could lead to declines in local populations of birds.

The authors suggest implementing a more gradual approach to controlling such nonnative shrubs: removing reproductive exotic shrubs first, planting native shrubs, and then removing nonreproductive shrubs.

Wilson, Scott D. 1989. The suppression of native prairie by alien species introduced for revegetation. Landscape and Urban Planning. 17: 113 119.

Annotation: This study examined the effect of using introduced vegetation for revegetating prairies disturbed by military tank traffic. It specifically sought to determine whether the use of commercial seed mixtures containing introduced species known to increase soil stability and nitrification would promote the long term recovery of native vegetation. The author compared the vegetation on unseeded plots of disturbed native prairie with plots seeded with commercial mixtures containing various quantities of exotics. The native flora was suppressed on seeded plots. Plots seeded with mixtures containing larger quantities of exotics contained the lowest frequency of native species, while unseeded plots contained the fewest exotics and the greatest total frequency of native species. In addition, naturally regenerating native vegetation was as efficient as seed mixtures at producing plant biomass and was more efficient at covering bare ground. The author concludes that native perennials are capable of revegetating disturbed prairie, while seeding exotics in revegetation efforts suppresses the native vegetation and does not produce more plant material than does natural regeneration.

Zavaleta, Erika S.; Hobbs, Richard J. Mooney, Harold A. 2001. Viewing invasive species removal in a whole-ecosystem context. Trends in Ecology and Evolution. 16(8): 454 459.

Annotation: Although eradication is often the ultimate management goal, managers must consider the role invasive species may play in the functioning ecosystem. The removal of an established species rarely has little impact on other species, and removal, in fact, may be more harmful to native species if measures are not taken to address these impacts. The authors provide numerous examples of how species can interact in a community and the cascading effects eradication may have. When both exotic herbivores and plants have invaded a system, removing the invasive plant may result in increased herbivory on native plants, potentially driving rare plants to extinction. As another consideration, species such as *Tamarix* have become so dominant in altered riparian systems that the endangered southwestern willow flycatcher (*Empidonax trailii extimus*) preferentially nests in the invasive species. Without addressing the anthropogenic changes that permitted the invasion of *Tamarix* (low water tables, high salinity, reduced flooding disturbance), reestablishment of native species used by nesting flycatchers (for example, cottonwoods [*Populus* spp.] and willows [*Salix* spp.]) is unlikely. Therefore, management should shift emphasis from invasive species eradication in natural systems and consider the broader emphasis of ecosystem restoration.

IV. Additional Resources

A. Sample Environmental Impact Statements (EIS)

Environmental Impact Statements (EIS) are prepared as a result of the National Environmental Policy Act (NEPA), when Federal agencies recognize that management actions or deci sions have the potential for significant environmental effects. The following documents are examples of EISs that specifi cally address the issue of managing weeds in wilderness. We found these by querying an Internet search engine with the terms "wilderness weed eis," "blm weed eis," "nps weed eis," "fws weed eis," and "usfws weed eis." Several relevant EISs, such as the Helena National Forest Weed Treatment Project and more general National Forest Land Management Plans and National Park Service or Bureau of Land Management Resource Management Plans, were in progress at the time of publication. While we have not assessed the quality of the analyses presented here, we offer them as examples of the types of issues that arise, and the types of analyses that have been conducted by Federal agencies attempting to manage invasive plants in and near designated wilderness, Wilderness Study Areas, and roadless areas.

U.S. Department of Agriculture, Forest Service, Bitterroot National Forest. 2002. Draft Environmental Impact State-ment: Noxious Weed Treatment Project. 202 p. + figures and 2 Appendices. (*Note: This document can be obtained from Bitterroot National Forest, Stevensville Ranger District Of fice, Stevensville, Montana, 59870; 406 777 5461 or online at http://www.fs.fed.us/r1/bitterroot/range/bitterweedeis.pdf.*)

Annotation: The Bitterroot National Forest drafted an envi ronmental impact statement (EIS) to treat noxious weeds on 35,000 acres, of which 5,000 acres are considered high risk areas following the 2000 fires. The EIS divides weed treat ment objectives into three categories, eradication, suppression, and containment, to guide management intensity and dura tion. For each invasive species found on the Forest (for ex ample, spotted knapweed, Canada thistle, tall buttercup, common tansy, sulfur cinquefoil, St. Johnswort, and oxeye daisy are all found in wilderness), the EIS assigns one of these categories as a management goal. The alternatives affect the

ability of managers to attain these goals, so a species targeted for eradication under one alternative, may be moved to the suppression or containment category depending on the tools available to managers under other alternatives. The EIS also presents results of previously approved treatments and pilot projects in a table of weed management methods including limitations, effectiveness, and cost. The proposed action (Al ternative A) includes aerial and ground based herbicide ap plication, biological control, cultural, and mechanical control, and education and prevention management techniques. Alter native B eliminates aerial application, and Alternative C pro poses similar actions without use of herbicides. Alternative D is a no action alternative. Because the treatment area affects wilderness, the Forest carefully considers the impacts actions may have on wilderness mandates. Specifically, the introduc tion of herbicides (proposed action and Alternative B) and bio logical control agents (proposed action and Alternatives B and C) would diminish wilderness experiences in the short term, but weed infestations continuing unchecked may have long term impacts on these experiences. In addition, the proposed action gives high priority to treating wilderness trails and trailheads. Because this a draft, the final EIS may change based on public comment.

U.S. Department of Agriculture, Forest Service, Inter-mountain and Northern Regions, Bitterroot, Nez Perce, Payette, and Salmon-Challis National Forests. 1999. Frank Church-River of No Return Wilderness noxious weed treat-ments: Environmental impact statement. 335 p. + 20 p. Record of Decision. (*To obtain a copy of this document con tact: Salmon and Challis National Forest, P.O. Box 729, Salmon, ID 83467; or Salmon River Ranger District, Box 70 HC01, White Bird, ID 83534.*)

Annotation: This environmental impact statement (EIS) out lines management actions to treat weed species prior to comple tion of the final comprehensive EIS for the Frank Church River of No Return Wilderness. At least 300 different sites repre senting 1,775 acres, which make up less than 1 percent of the wilderness area, are proposed for treatment of noxious weed infestations. Species of greatest concern include sulfur cinque foil, spotted knapweed, rush skeletonweed, yellow starthistle, Dyer's woad, and dalmatian toadflax. The majority of infesta tions in this wilderness occur along the major rivers. This EIS compares five alternatives including: Alternative 1   no change from the current management of sporadic weed pulling with no monitoring; Alternative 2   a combination of manual, bio logical, and chemical practices to treat weeds throughout the wilderness; Alternative 3   a less aggressive treatment simi lar to Alternative 2; Alternative 4   a treatment similar to Al ternative 2 but only along major river corridors; and Alternative 5   use of manual and biological controls only. The proposed action (Alternative 2) is designed to reduce the rate of spread of noxious weeds through: (1) a combination of manual, chemi cal, and biological methods; (2) implementing restoration fol lowing control methods; and (3) monitoring. In addition, the EIS discusses Integrated Weed Management and Minimum Tool principles as applied to the proposed action and the alter natives. The EIS includes maps of infestations and areas sus ceptible to invasion as well as the current management directions of the four Forests that administer the wilderness. The EIS also describes the environmental consequences of the alternatives as they relate to wilderness directives and wil derness values in terms of both potential weed expansion and treatment impacts.

U.S. Department of the Interior, Bureau of Land Manage-ment. 1991. Final environmental impact statement: Veg-etation treatment on BLM lands in thirteen western states. 327 p. + 14 appendices + 17 p. Record of Decision. (*Note: This document can be obtained online at http://www.blm.gov/ weeds/VegEIS or by contacting BLM Wyoming State Office at 307 775 6256.*)

Annotation: This final environmental impact statement (FEIS) examines the impacts of weed control methods on Bureau of Land Management lands in 13 Western States (Arizona, Colo rado, Idaho, Montana, Nevada, New Mexico, North Dakota, Oklahoma, eastern Oregon, South Dakota, Utah, Washington, and Wyoming) including 416,000 acres of wilderness or wil derness study area designation administered by the Bureau. Rather than address site specific impacts, however, the FEIS uses broad regional characteristics to describe the general impacts that might result from the alternatives and the pro posed action. The analysis uses 14 resource components (veg etation, climate and air quality, geography and topography, soils, aquatic resources, fish and wildlife, cultural resources, recreation and visual resources, livestock, wild horses and burros, special status species, wilderness and special areas, human health and safety, and social and economic resources) and considers how impacts may vary across vegetation types (sagebrush, desert shrub, Southwestern shrub steppe, chapar ral mountain shrub, pinyon juniper, Plains grassland, moun tain/plateau grassland, and coniferous/deciduous forest). Because wilderness areas are considered only as one resource component, the FEIS does not address how the alternatives impact wilderness but rather how the alternatives affect man agement options for the BLM wildernesses. The FEIS ad dresses the short and long term impacts and the cumulative effects that treatment by the BLM in conjunction with other agencies and individuals may have on both natural and hu man environments. The proposed action is an expansion of current management practices and allows the use of all avail able treatment methods (including manual, mechanical, bio logical, chemical, and fire) to treat a maximum of 372,000 acres of the total 156 million acres controlled by the Bureau

in these States. Alternative 2 considers management actions without the use of aerial application of herbicides, whereas Alternative 3 analyses management without using herbicides at all. Alternative 4 considers impacts without the use of pre scribed burning. Continuation of current management is con sidered under Alternative 5. In addition to the Standard Operating Procedures used to treat vegetation, which are de scribed in the first chapter, the 14 appendices provide exten sive information including the details of nonchemical treatment methods (Appendix C), risk assessments associated with pre scribed burning (Appendix D), application of 19 herbicides and two additives (Appendix E), and the fire ecology of West ern plants (Appendix F).

U.S. Department of the Interior, Bureau of Land Manage-ment. [Ongoing]. Environmental Impact Statement for Vegetation Treatments, Watersheds and Wildlife Habitats on Public Lands Administered by the BLM in the Western United States, Including Alaska. (*Note: Notes regarding the status of this document can be obtained online at http:// www.blm.gov/weeds/VegEIS.*)

Annotation: The BLM has initiated the process of develop ing a new EIS to evaluate proposed vegetation treatment al ternatives for 18 Western States, including Alaska. Once it is finalized, this EIS will supercede previous programmatic docu ments for the same geographic area, such as the BLM's FEIS listed here (USDI, BLM 1991). This updated EIS will respond to new policies and programs implemented by the BLM, new information about vegetation treatment methods and impacts, and revised BLM vegetation management objectives that in clude a substantial increase in the number of acres to be treated (6 million acres annually compared to 506,853 acres permit ted under the Record of Decisions from the previous EIS). A public scoping process was initiated by publishing a Notice of Intent in the Federal Register on January 22, 2002. Current information on the status of this document, including news releases and a summary of public comments, can be found on the BLM's Weeds Web site (*http://www.blm.gov/weeds/ VegEIS*).

B. Online Resources

There are a plethora of useful Web sites devoted to the is sues surrounding invasive plants. The first section highlights databases that include species lists, distribution records, regu latory information, control techniques, and the status and con trol of invasive species in wilderness. The second section represents a selected list of sites with pertinent invasive plant information, contacts, approaches to management, access to programs, and other resources. These sites are primarily U.S. based. State specific Web sites were generally not included. Each citation in this section is followed by the date we last accessed the home page.

1. Databases

CalWeed Database: California Noxious Weed Control Projects Inventory, [Online]. Available: http:// endeavor.des.ucdavis.edu/weeds [2002, July 31].

Annotation: This is a combined government/private/nonprofit effort to establish an Internet database that contains information on noxious weed control in California.

Database of Integrated Pest Management Resources, [Online]. Available: http://www.ippc.orst.edu/cicp/gateway/weed.htm [2002, July 31].

Annotation: This site provides access to an extensive compilation of Internet resources on weeds and their control (65 resources listed at time of press).

NPSpecies, [Online]. Available: http://www.nature.nps.gov/im/apps/npspp [2002, July 31].

Annotation: Developed and maintained by the National Park Service, this tool records park specific information about both plants and animals. For each species that occurs in a National Park, this database includes presence/absence, abundance, residency, nativity, whether the species is weedy, management and exploitation concerns, and preferred scientific and common names. Three additional lookup databases work with the NPSpecies application. They include a taxonomic module that provides a list of scientific names and common names and their linkages to synonyms as well as links to taxonomic hierarchies; a parks module that provides a standard list of park names, park State information, and Inventory and Monitoring Network information; and a Threatened and Endangered Species module. The latter provides lists of Federally listed species (from Fish and Wildlife Service [FWS] TESS data base), globally ranked species (from The Nature Conservancy, and State listed species (from individual State agencies).

PLANTS Database, [Online]. Available: http://plants.usda.gov [2002, July 31].

Annotation: Administered by the USDA Natural Resources Conservation Service, this is the USDA's single source of standardized information about plants. While this database is not limited to invasive species, it does contain Federal and State lists of noxious weeds. Focusing on vascular plants, mosses, liverworts, hornworts, and lichens of the United States and its Territories, the PLANTS database includes scientific and common names, checklists, automated tools, identification information, species abstracts, distributional data, crop information, plant symbols, plant growth data, plant materials information, plant links, references, and other plant information.

Southwest Exotic Mapping Program (SWEMP), [Online]. Available: http://usgssrv1.usgs.nau.edu/swepic/swemp/maps.html [2002, July 31].

Annotation: The master regional database, which is compiled by the USGS Colorado Plateau Field Station and housed on this site, contains exotic plant distributions for the Southwest (Arizona, New Mexico, and adjacent areas of adjoining States) and includes the ability to generate geographic information system based distribution maps. The regional database and collaborators manual are both available for download.

The Invaders Database System, [Online]. Available: http://invader.dbs.umt.edu [2002, July 31].

Annotation: This site consists of a comprehensive database of nonnative plant species, distribution records, and regulatory information for the Northwestern United States. Approximately 1,000 species and 80,000 distribution records are included. Historic distribution data starting as early as 1870

are available for certain species. The INVADERS software is available for download. Additionally, agency users that are taxonomically qualified can add new data on nonnative plants online as well as receive updated outputs, and users can sign up for the automated e mail alert system that will provide new reports of important noxious weeds. This site provides direct links to all State noxious weed lists and to other Web sites that post pictures, describe management, and provide ecological and other descriptive information on specific invasive species.

Wilderness Invaders Project, [Online]. Available: http://leopold.wilderness.net/research/invasives/invaders.htm [2002, July 31].

Annotation: This site provides access to two databases: one from a survey of exotic plants on Federally designated wilderness areas managed by the USDA Forest Service, USDI National Park Service, Fish and Wildlife Service, and the Bureau of Land Management, and a second that resulted from a survey of invasive and exotic species in wilderness managed by the Fish and Wildlife Service. The former, funded by the Leopold Institute and conducted in 1997 and 1998, consisted of a survey of wilderness area managers and resource specialists. The second database, funded by the Fish and Wildlife Service and conducted in 2001, also included animals and pathogens. The primary objectives of these surveys were to document both the occurrence of nonnative plant species in wilderness areas and the various control efforts being used to combat them. The databases include contact information for the responding wilderness areas and information on the various species invading these areas (species names, patterns of infestation, control methods, and so forth). Both databases can be downloaded from this site.

2. Other Online Resources

Aldo Leopold Wilderness Research Institute, [Online]. Available: http://leopold.wilderness.net [2002, July 31].

Annotation: This site is the Homepage of the Leopold Institute, a Federal interagency research group that provides scientific leadership to sustain wilderness. The Leopold Institute has identified nonnative species as one of its three priority research issues. This reading list as well others in the Linking Wilderness Research and Management Series are available through this Web site.

Alien Plants Ranking System, [Online]. Available: http://usgssrv1.usgs.nau.edu/swepic/aprs/ranking.html [2002, July 31].

Annotation: This Web site provides a link to download the Alien Plant Ranking System (APRS), a user friendly computer program designed to help land managers prioritize decisions concerning invasive plants. APRS can help to focus limited resources and target those species likely to cause major impacts or threats to resources or those that impede attainment of management goals. It provides an analytical tool to separate the innocuous species from the invasive ones and can identify species with high future impact potential. The system addresses the feasibility of control of each species, enabling the manager to weigh the costs of control against the level of impact. The system relies on a set of questions to be answered for each nonnative plant known to occur in or near the site of concern.

American Lands Alliance Invasive Species Page, [Online]. Available: http://www.americanlands.org/forestweb/invasive.htm [2002, July 31].

Annotation: This site, hosted by American Lands Alliance, provides information about the threat of noxious weeds in wild areas and provides links to many useful Web sites and reports or documents.

Animal and Plant Health Inspection Service's Noxious Weeds Homepage, [Online]. Available: http://www.aphis.usda.gov/ppq/weeds [2002, July 31].

Annotation: In addition to APHIS specific weed information and fact sheets, this site provides links to Federal and State noxious weed lists. APHIS seeks to prevent and control noxious weeds detrimental to U.S. agriculture and the environment in general.

Bureau of Land Management's Weeds Web site, [Online]. Available: http://www.blm.gov/weeds [2002, July 31].

Annotation: This Web site provides information regarding invasive weeds from the BLM's perspective. Included are links to BLM State weed sites, BLM contacts, the BLM's national strategy for invasive plant management, and species specific "weed wanted posters."

California Exotic Pest Plant Council (CalEPPC), [Online]. Available: http://www.caleppc.org [2002, August 6].

Annotation: With a membership including land managers, consultants, scientists, planners, nonprofit organizations and volunteers, the California Exotic Pest Plant Council (CalEPPC) is a California based organization that proposes and facilitates solutions for people who are interested in the protection, management, and enjoyment of California's natural areas and who have concerns over the alarming spread of invasive exotic vegetation. Their Web site provides publication information, access to their newsletters, book reviews, information about combating invasive brooms, and a pest plant list that highlights nonnative plants that pose serious problems in California's wildlands. CalEPPC conducts an annual symposium, and their Web site provides access to past symposia proceedings. The Web site also includes links to other useful sites, including other EPPC Web sites, pest plant information in California and other States, Federal Web sites, organizational Web sites, and Web sites with information on restoration and weed control.

Center for Invasive Plant Management, [Online]. Available: http://www.weedcenter.org [2002, July 31].

Annotation: CIPM, based at Montana State University, represents a coalition of government agencies, organizations, and individuals interested in managing invasive plants and maintaining ecosystems in Western North America. The Center's goals are to enhance education, coordinate regional research, facilitate partnerships, increase multidisciplinary communication, and implement practical management. This Web site provides weed fact sheets, and other educational information geared toward land managers, and extensive links to State, Province, and other governmental sites.

Exotic Plant Management Teams, [Online]. Available: http://www.nature.nps.gov/epmt [2002, July 31].

Annotation: See section III.E.1. Page 42.

Extoxnet: Extension Toxicology Network, [Online]. Available: http://pmep.cce.cornell.edu/profiles/extoxnet/index.html [2002, July 31].

Annotation: This is the Web site of the Pesticide Information Project of the cooperative extension offices of Cornell University, Michigan State University, Oregon State University, and University of California at Davis with support provided by the USDA Extension Service, National Agricultural Pesticide Impact Assessment Program. Information on specific herbicides is available.

Federal Interagency Committee for the Management of Noxious and Exotic Weeds (FICMNEW), [Online]. Available: http://ficmnew.fws.gov [2002, July 31].

Annotation: FICMNEW's Homepage provides information about this committee and access to the Federal invasive species executive order (Presidential Executive Order 13112), the National Strategy for Invasive Plant Management, which is the Federal strategic overview intended to highlight successful ways to battle invasive plants, workshops, meeting dates and agendas, an online version of the "weed fact book" and other resources, and links to members.

Global Invasive Species Program, [Online]. Available: http://jasper.stanford.edu/GISP [2002, July 31].

Annotation: This is an international, interdisciplinary program with a proactive approach to prevention and management of invasive species. This Web site details their strategies and provides links to publications, meetings, and specific strategies.

Handbook for Ranking Exotic Plants for Management and Control, [Online]. Available: http://www1.nature.nps.gov/pubs/ranking [2002, July 31].

Annotation: This site provides access to an online version of R. D. Hiebert and J. Stubbendieck's 1993 handbook. Developed by the USDI National Park Service, this handbook consists of a ranking system to help resource managers prioritize which exotic plants they should target for control efforts. See full annotation in section III.C. Page 37.

Invasive Plants of Canada Council, [Online]. Available: http://infoweb.magi.com/~ehaber/ipcan.html [2002, July 31].

Annotation: Includes links to information sources and fact sheets as well as the online version of Invasive Plants of Canada: Guide to Species and Methods of Control.

Invasivespecies.gov, [Online]. Available: http://www.invasivespecies.gov [2002, July 31].

Annotation: This comprehensive U.S. government site is the gateway to Federal efforts concerning invasive species. It includes information regarding the impacts of invasives, the government's response, profiles of selected species, and links to other agencies and organizations. The National Invasive Species Council, also accessed through this Web site, coordinates responses to the problems associated with invasives. The site contains links to agency Web sites, Presidential Executive Order 13112, and the national invasive species management plan entitled "Meeting the Invasive Species Challenge." Also see section III.A. Page 34.

Southeast Exotic Pest Plant Council (SE-EPPC), [Online]. Available: http://www.se eppc.org [2002, August 7].

Annotation: A nonprofit organization, the Southeast Exotic Pest Plant Council strives to increase public awareness about the spread of exotic plants, facilitate the regional exchange of information about invasive plant management and control, provide a forum for exchange through meetings, workshops and symposia, provide educational, advisory, and technical support on exotic plant issues, and initiate campaign actions to prevent future invasions. This is an umbrella organization with links to each Southeastern State's EPPC Web site. It also links to the National EPPC Web site.

Southwest Exotic Plant Information Clearinghouse (SWEPIC), [Online]. Available: http://usgssrv1.usgs.nau.edu/swepic [2002, July 31].

Annotation: A cooperative effort among the U.S. Geological Survey, the National Park Service and Northern Arizona University, the Southwest Exotic Plant Information Clearinghouse organizes information on exotic plant species in the Southwest into a single Web location. The SWEPIC's goal is to provide reliable and organized information on the distribution and ecology of weeds in the Southwest, with an emphasis on forests, rangelands, and other natural areas. This site houses the Southwest Exotic Mapping Program (see description under IV.B.1., page 57), the Alien Plant Ranking System (see description in this section, page 57), links to information about weed species that occur in the Southwest, as well as noxious weed lists and watch lists for species that are considered to be of special concern but are not yet designated as legally noxious.

The Nature Conservancy's Wildland Invasive Species Program (Weeds on the Web), [Online]. Available: http://tncweeds.ucdavis.edu [2002, July 31].

Annotation: This Web site provides access to TNC's weed management library with many resources for individual invasive species (including their "Elemental Stewardship Abstracts" for specific plant species). Also from this site, TNC'S extensive "Weed Control Methods Handbook: Tools and Techniques for Use in Natural Areas" can be downloaded (in increments or in its entirety).

Weeds Gone Wild: Alien Plant Invaders of Natural Areas, [Online]. Available: http://www.nps.gov/plants/alien [2002, July 31].

Annotation: This Web site is a product of the Plant Conservation Alliance's Alien Plant Working Group. It provides information on the problem of invasive species, fact sheets that include plant descriptions, native range, U.S. distribution and habitat, management options, suggested alternative native plants, and other information. It also includes selected links to relevant people and organizations.

C. Cooperative Weed Management Areas

Crossing ownership boundaries, Cooperative Weed Management Areas consist of city, county, State, and Federal land managers as well as private landowners, conservation groups, and community groups who coordinate efforts and expertise against invasive weed species within given geographic areas. These groups collaborate to address both "wildland" weeds and agricultural weeds. Different weed management areas are initiated and/or governed by members or boards representing different entities. The following list includes guidelines, for the coordinated management of noxious weeds within weed management areas, that were developed for 14 Western States, as well as an example Web site representing California's progressive network of cooperative weed management areas.

California's Weed Management Areas, [Online]. Available: http://www.cdfa.ca.gov/phpps/ipc/weedmgtareas/Index.html [2002, July 31].

Annotation: California has an extensive Web site addressing the State's cooperative weed management area efforts. In addition to listing contacts for all of the California weed management areas, this site has information about weed events, education, funding sources, legislation, Statewide meetings, newsletters, and specific projects.

Free, Jim; Mullin, Barbra; McNeel, Hank; Parsons, Robert; McClure, Craig. 1999. Guidelines for Coordinated Management of Noxious Weeds: Development of Weed Management Areas. USDI Bureau of Land Management: Billings, MT. 228 p. (*Note: The guidelines are available online at http://www.team.ars.usda.gov/.*)

Annotation: These guidelines provide a working document for developing weed management programs within specific Weed Management Areas. In addition to describing the purpose and organization of weed management areas, this document covers the major components of weed management programs (for example, education, prevention, mapping, integrated weed management, monitoring, and management plans). Appendices include sample contracts and agreements, State and Federal noxious weed laws, weed free forage certification standards, public meeting guidelines, sample questionnaires and reporting forms, monitoring techniques, databases, site assessment worksheets, and funding sources.

AUTHOR INDEX

Multiple page number listings result from works cited in more than one section of the document. For articles that ap pear more than once, an * marks the page containing the an notation.

Abbott 1992   page 24
Allendorf and others 2001   page 13
Anderson and others 1977   page 29
Anderson and Wotring 2001   pages 33, 41*
Aplet 1990   page 24
Asher and Harmon 1995   page 5
Asher and others 2001   page 35
Ashton and Mitchell 1989   pages 13*, 42

Baker 1986   pages 9*, 14
Baker and Mickelson 1994   page 48
Barrett 1992   page 13
Barrows 1993   page 52
Baskin 2002   page 9
Bazzaz 1986   page 14
Bedunah and Carpenter 1989   page 48
Benninger-Truax and others 1992   pages 22*, 39
Berger 1993   page 53
Binggeli 1996   page 9
Blossey and others 2001   page 45
Bock and Bock 1992   page 51
Bock and others 1986   page 29
Bossard 1991   page 15
Brandt and Rickard 1994   page 15*, 29
Bratton 1982   page 5
Briese 1996   pages 15*, 45
Brooks and Pyke 2001   pages 15, 24*
Brothers and Spingarn 1992   page 15
Brown and others 2001   page 39
Burke and Grime 1996   pages 14, 15*
Burns and Sauer 1992   page 15
Bussan and Dyer 1999   page 49

Cadenasso and Pickett 2001   page 16
Callaway and Aschehoug 2000   page 14
Cameron and Spencer 1989   page 25
Campbell 2001   page 35
Cheater 1992   page 5
Chicoine and others 1985   page 37
Cione and others 2002   page 53
Cole and Landres 1996   page 5
Colton and Alpert 1998   page 42
Cox 1999   page 9
Crawley 1987   pages 16*, 22
Cronk and Fuller 1995   page 10

D'Antonio and Vitousek 1992   page 25
Daehler and Strong 1996   pages 35*, 37
Davis and others 2000   page 16
Deering and Vankat 1998   page 22
DeLoach 1997   page 45
Dewey and others 1991   pages 37*, 39
Disney and Stokes 1976   page 29
Donald 1994   page 39
Drake and others 1989   page 10
Dudley and Collins 1995   page 5
Dudley and Embury 1995   pages 6*, 16

Ellis 1995   page 29
Ellis and others 1997   page 29
Elton 1958   page 10
Everitt and others 1995   page 40
Everitt and others 1996   page 39

Fay 1992   page 49
Floyd-Hanna and others 1993   page 16
Follett and Duan 2000   page 45
Forcella and Harvey 1983   page 16
Free and others 1999   page 59
Fuller and Barbe 1985   pages 42, 50*

Galley and Wilson 2001   page 16
Gassmann and Louda 2001   page 45
Germano and others 2001   page 51
Goodwin and others 1999   page 37
Gordon 1998   page 25
Grace and others 2001   page 17*, 25
Greenberg and others 1997   pages 17*, 22
Groves 1989   page 42
Groves and others 2001   pages 37*, 42

Harris 1988   page 46
Hastings and DiTomaso 1996   page 51
Hester 1991   page 6
Hester and Hobbs 1992   page 17
Heywood 1989   pages 10*, 22
Hiebert 1997   pages 33*, 42
Hiebert and Stubbendieck 1993   page 37*, 42
Higgins and others 1999   page 37
Higgins and others 2001   page 37
Hitchmough and others 1994   page 49
Hobbs 1989   page 17
Hobbs 1991   page 17
Hobbs and Huenneke 1992   page 18
Hobbs and Humphries 1995   page 33
Hoshovsky and Randall 2000   page 42
Howarth 1991   page 46
Huenneke 1996   page 25
Huenneke and others 1990   page 18
Hughes and others 1991   page 18*, 25
Hunter and others   page 29

Jacobs and others 1999   page 53
Johansson and others 1996   page 22
Johnson 1999   page 40

Johnson and others 1994   page 30
Johnstone 1986   page 18

Keeley 2001   pages 18*, 25, 51
Kowarik 1995   page 38
Kummerow 1992   pages 6*, 35

Lacey and Olson 1991   page 10
Lacey and others 1992   pages 22, 51*
Lachowski and others 1996   page 40
Lake and others 1997   page 40
Lambrinos 2000   pages 26*, 30
Lass and Callihan 1993   page 40
Lesica and others 1993   page 6
Levine 2000   page 19
Levine and D'Antonio 1999   page 19
Ley and D'Antonio 1998   page 26
Litt and others 2001   page 49
Lodge 1993   page 38
Lonsdale 1999   page 19
Lonsdale and Lane 1994   page 22
Loope 1992   page 6
Loope and others 1988   page 6
Louda 1998   page 46
Louda and others 1997   page 46
Luken and Thieret 1997   page 10
Lyons and Schwartz 2001   page 19

Macdonald and Frame 1988   pages 7*, 19, 26, 30
Macdonald and others 1988   page 7
Macdonald and others 1989   pages 7, 26*, 30
Mack 1984   page 19
Mack 1989   page 19
Mack 1996   page 38
Mack and D'Antonio 1998   page 26
Mack and Lonsdale 2001   page 22
Madsen 1997   pages 33*, 43
Marcus and others 1998   pages 23*, 40
Marion and others 1986   page 7
Marler 2000   7
Marrs and Lowday 1984   page 49
Mayes and others 1987   page 49
Mazzotti and others 1981   page 30
McArthur and others 1990   page 26
McCarthy 1997   page 50
Milberg and Lamont 1995   page 20
Monsen and Kitchen 1994   page 11
Moody and Mack 1988   page 43
Mooney and Cleland 2001   page 26
Mooney and Drake 1986   page 11
Mooney and Hobbs 2000   page 11
Morrison 1997   page 53
Mortensen 1986   page 46
Mullin 1992   page 43

National Invasive Species Council 2001   page 34
Novak and Mack 2001   page 23

Office of Technology Assessment 1993   page 11

Olson 1999a   pages 11*, 27
Olson 1999b   page 51
Orians 1986   page 20

Panetta and Mitchell 1991   page 38
Pearson and Ortega 2001   page 23
Pearson and others 2000   page 46
Pearson and others 2001   page 30
Pemberton 2000   page 47
Peters and Bunting 1994   page 27
Pieterse and Murphy 1990   pages 11, 43*
Pimentel and others 2000   page 12
Post and others 1990   page 52
Prather and Callihan 1993   pages 41*, 43
Pyle 1995   page 20

Randall 1993   page 43
Randall 1995   page 7
Randall 1996   pages 7*, 27, 43
Randall 1997   pages 12*, 43
Randall 2000   page 8
Randall and others 2001   page 43
Reichard 1997   pages 36, 38*
Reichard and Hamilton 1997   pages 14, 38*
Reichard and White 2001   page 36
Rejmánek 1996   page 14
Rejmánek and Richardson 1996   pages 14*, 39
Reynolds 1979   page 30
Ricciardi and others 2000   page 34
Rice and Toney 1998   page 49
Rice and others 1997a   page 30
Rice and others 1997b   page 50
Richardson and others 1994   pages 14*, 20
Richardson and others 2000   page 12
Richburg and others 2001   page 27
Robinson and others 1995   page 20
Rosen 1982   page 53
Roundy and others 1995   page 53

Sallabanks 1993   page 23
Schaffner 2001   page 47
Schiffman 1997   page 23
Schmidt and Whelan 1999   page 30
Schmitz and Simberloff 2001   pages 36*, 44
Schmitz and others 1993   pages 27*, 44
Schwaller 2001   page 34
Schwartz 1997   page 34
Schwartz and Randall 1995   pages 34*, 44
Self 1986   page 41
Sheldon and Creed 1995   page 47
Sheley and Petroff 1999   page 34
Sheley and others 1999a   page 36
Sheley and others 1999b   page 44
Sher and others 2000   page 53
Simberloff and Stiling 1996   page 47
Simberloff and Von Holle 1999   pages 20*, 27
Slobodchikoff and Doyen 1977   pages 27, 31*
Stapanian and others 1998   pages 12, 21*

Steenkamp and Chown 1996   pages 27, 31*
Stelljes and Wood 2000   page 47
Stohlgren and others 1998   pages 21*, 41
Stohlgren and others 1999a   page 21
Stohlgren and others 1999b   page 21
Story 1992   page 47
Strobel 1991   page 47
Stromayer and others 1998   page 31
Suszkiw 2000   page 50

Thompson 1996   page 31
Thomsen and others 1993   page 52
Trammell and Butler 1995   page 31
Tu and others 2001   pages 44*, 50, 51, 52
Tucker and Richardson 1995   page 39
Tyser and Worley 1992   page 23
Tyser and others 1998   pages 50*, 54

U.S. Department of Agriculture 2000   page 48
U.S. Department of Agriculture, Forest Service 1999   page 55
U.S. Department of Agriculture, Forest Service 2002   page 55
U.S. Department of Interior, Bureau of Land
    Management 1991   pae 56
U.S. Department of Interior, Bureau of Land
    Management [Ongoing]   page 56
Usher 1988   page 8

Van Driesche and Van Driesche 2001   page 36
Vellend 2002   page 24
Vitousek 1986   page 27
Vitousek 1992   page 28
Vitousek and others 1987   page 28
Vitousek and others 1996   page 12

Wadsworth and others 2000   pages 39, 44*
Walker and Smith 1997   pages 28*, 54
Wallander and others 1995   page 52
Wapshere 1974   page 48
Weaver and Woods 1986   page 21
Westbrooks 1998   page 12
Westman 1990   pages 44, 54*
Whelan and Dilger 1992   pages 31, 44, 54*
Whisenant 1990   page 28
Willard and others 1988   page 31
Williams 1997   page 50
Williams and Karl 1997   page 31
Wilson 1989   page 54
Wilson and Belcher 1989   page 32
Wilson and McCaffrey 1999   page 48
Woods 1997   pages 14, 28*
Wright and Kelsey 1997   page 32

Zamora and Thill 1999   pages 41*, 44
Zamora and others 1989   page 44
Zavaleta 2000   page 45

INDEX OF PLANTS AND SELECTED VEGETATION TYPES

Although the reading list does not address individual species or vegetation types comprehensively, this index will help readers locate papers of interest. Some authors did not refer to both scientific and common names. As a result, readers may want to check the index under both the common and scientific names. Additionally, plant names are listed as they appear in the original publications and may not reflect current taxonomy. Readers can refer to the U.S. Department of Agriculture's PLANTS database (http://plants.usda.gov/cgi bin) for a current, standardized list of common and scientific plant names.

Agropyron spp.   page 20
   cirstatum   page 30
Alliaria petiolata   page 50
Ammophila arenaria   pages 27, 31
aquatic   pages 6, 7, 10, 11, 13, 27, 28, 33, 42, 43, 44, 47
Artemisia tridentata   page 30
Avena fatua   page 53

barberry, Japanese   page 27
Berberis thunbergii   page 27
Betula spp.   page 49
birch   page 49
Bouteloua spp.   page 16
brome, red   page 25
Bromus madritensis   page 25
   tectorum   pages 15, 17, 19, 23, 25, 26, 27, 28
   (see also cheatgrass)
broom, scotch   page 15
buckthorn, glossy   page 52
bunchgrass   pages 18, 30, 32
buttercup, tall   page 55

Carduus spp.   page 46
   (see also thistle, musk)
Casuarina equisetifolia   page 30
Centaurea spp.   page 47
   biebersteinii   page 17
   (see also *C. maculosa*)
   diffusa   pages 14, 35
   maculosa   pages 17, 23, 30, 31, 32, 37, 40, 46, 48, 49, 50, 52
   repens   page 30
   solstitialis   pages 40, 51, 52
   virgata   page 35
   (also see listings under knapweed, starthistle)
chaparral   pages 15, 18, 26, 56

cheatgrass   pages 12, 15, 17, 19, 23, 25, 26, 27, 28
   (see also *Bromus tectorum*)
Chondrilla juncea   pages 35, 40
cinquefoil, sulfur   page 55
Cirsium spp.   pages 45, 46, 47
   arvense   pages 5, 39
   (also see listings under thistle)
Clintonia spp.   page 21
conifer   pages 15, 17, 18, 56
   (also see listings under pine, *Pinus*, *Pseudotsuga*, *Sequoiadendron*, *Thuja*, *Tsuga*)
cordgrass   pages 35, 37
Cortaderia jubata   pages 26, 30
cottonwood   pages 29, 54
   (also see listings under *Populus*)
Crataegus monogyna   page 23
crupina, common   pages 40, 41
Crupina vulgaris   pages 40, 41
Cytisus scoparius   page 15

daisy, oxeye   page 55
desert,   pages 11, 12, 15, 17, 18, 19, 24, 25, 28, 35, 51, 52, 56
   Chihuahuan   page 42
   Sonoran   page 25
Douglas-fir   page 16
dune   pages 14, 27, 31

Eichhornia spp.   page 5
   crassipes   page 27
Elaeagnus angustifolia   page 27
Eragrostis curvula   page 29
   lehmanniana   pages 29, 53
   (also see listings under lovegrass)
Erodium cicutarium   page 25
Eschscholzia californica   page 20
Eucalyptus spp.   page 54
Euphorbia esula   pages 17, 31, 40, 51

fayatree   page 28
   (see also *Myrica faya*)
fern, bracken   page 49
fescue,   pages 49, 50
   tall   page 5
Festuca arundinacea   page 5
filaree, red-stemmed   page 25
forest,   pages 9, 10, 12, 14, 15, 16, 20, 21, 22, 24, 25, 26, 28, 29, 31, 32, 34, 35, 37, 48, 50
   coniferous   pages 17, 18, 56
   deciduous   pages 16, 17, 56
   rainforest   page 24
   subtropical   page 42
   tropical   page 26

grass,   pages 11, 14, 17, 18, 19, 25, 26, 27, 28, 29, 31, 32, 36, 41, 48, 49, 50, 51, 52, 53
   barnyard   page 13

beach   page 31
cheat (see cheatgrass)
mediterranean   pages 7, 25
tussock   pages 20, 26
    (also see listings under *Agryopyron, Bouteloua,*
    brome, bunchgrass, cordgrass, *Bromus, Festuca,*
    grassland, shortgrass, ryegrass, wheatgrass)
grassland   pages 10, 13, 14, 16, 17, 18, 19, 20, 21,
    23, 24, 25, 26, 27, 29, 31, 35, 41, 42, 46, 49, 51, 52,
    56

hawthorn   page 23
honeysuckle,   24
    Amur   page 22
    (also see listings under *Lonicera*)
hyacinth, water   pages 5, 13, 27
hydrilla   page 27
Hydrilla verticillata   page 27
Hypericum perforatum   pages 15, 46
    (see also St. Johnswort)

Isatis tinctoria   pages 37, 39
    (see also woad)

knapweed,
    diffuse   pages 14, 35, 47
    Russian   page 30
    spotted   pages 17, 23, 30, 31, 32, 37, 40, 46, 47,
    48, 49, 50, 52, 55
    squarrose   page 35
    (also see listings under *Centaurea*)
Kochia spp.   page 20
kudzu   pages 12, 53

lantana, ornamental   page 46
Lantana camara   page 46
lettuce, water   page 27
Ligustrum sinense   page 31
Lolium temulentum   page 19
Lonicera spp.   page 24
    maackii   pages 22, 30
loosestrife, purple   pages 12, 45
lovegrass,
    African   page 51
    Boer   page 29
    Lehmann   pages 29, 53
Lythrum salicaria   page 45
    (see also purple loosestrife)

medusahead   page 27
melaleuca   page 12
Melaleuca quinquenervia   page 30
mesquite   page 31
mimosa   page 9
mustard, garlic   page   page 50
Myrica faya   pages 24, 28
Myriophyllum spicatum   page 47

nutsedge, purple   page 12

oats, wild   page 53
olive, Russian   page 27
Oplopanax spp.   page 21

pea   page 9
pine,   pages 9, 14, 15, 17, 20, 49
    Australian   page 30
    Monterey   page 29
    ponderosa   page 18
    (also see listings under *Pinus, Casuarina*)
Pinus spp.   page 14
    ponderosa   pages 16, 18
    radiata   page 29
pinyon-juniper   page 56
Pistia stratiotes   page 27
poppy, California   page 20
Populus spp.   page 54
    deltoids   pages 53, 54
    fremontii   page 29
    (see also cottonwood)
Potentilla spp.   page 47
privet, Chinese   page 31
Prosopis glandulosa   pages 27, 31
Pseudotsuga menziesii   page 16
Pteridium aquilinium   page 49
Pueraria lobata   page 53

ragwort, arrowleaf   page 47
rainforest   page 24
Rhamnus cathartica   page 30
    frangula   page 52
riparian   pages 6, 21, 22, 29, 39, 41, 44, 45, 52, 54
rose   page 9
ryegrass   page 53

sagebrush,   pages 28, 56
    big   pages 26, 27, 30
Salix spp.   page 54
saltcedar   pages 17, 28, 29, 39, 45, 54
    (also see listings under tamarisk, *Tamarix*)
Sapium sebiferum   page 25
savanna   pages 19, 27, 30, 31
Schismus spp.   page 25
Senecio triangularis   page 47
sequoia, giant   page 18
Sequoiadendron giganteum   page 18
skeletonweed, rush   pages 35, 40, 55
shortgrass   page 42
shrub-steppe   pages 15, 29, 56
    (see also sagebrush)
shrubland,   pages 14, 17, 18, 53
    desert   pages 25, 56
    mediterranean   pages 26, 30, 39, 42
    (see also chaparral)
Spartina spp.   pages 35, 37

spurge, leafy   pages 17, 22, 31, 40, 47, 51
    (see also *Euphorbia*)
St. Johnswort   pages 15, 46, 47, 55
starthistle, yellow   pages 12, 40, 51, 52, 55
    (see also *Centraurea*)
Stipa spp.   page 16

Taeniatherum caput-medusae   page 27
tallow, Chinese   page 17
tallow tree, Chinese   page 25
tamarisk,   pages 12, 28, 45, 52
    Chinese   page 39
    (also see listings under saltcedar, *Tamarix*)
Tamarix spp.   pages 6, 11, 17, 28, 45, 54
    chinensis   pages 29, 39
    ramosissima   pages 52, 53, 54
    (also see listings under saltcedar, tamarisk)
tansy, common   page 55
thistle,   pages 16, 45, 46, 47
    Canada   pages 5, 39, 55
    musk   pages 16, 46
    (also see listings under *Carduus, Cirsium*)
Thuja spp.   page 21
toadflax, dalmatian   pages 47, 55
tree, paperbark   page 30
Triadica sebifera   page 17
Tsuga spp.   page 21

watermilfoil, Eurasian   page 47
wheatgrass, crested   page 30
willow   pages 29, 54
woad, Dyer's   pages 37, 39, 55
woodland,   pages 7, 8, 26, 30, 31, 42
    pine-oak   pages 15, 17, 18, 19
    pinyon-juniper   page 56

Rocky Mountain Research Station
240 West Prospect Road
Fort Collins, CO 80526